ROB CUESTA

Authority!

How Experts Just Like You
Are Using **Authority Books**
To Grow Their Influence,
Raise Their Fees
And Steal Your Clients!

Rob Cuesta

The Income Accelerator For Professional Experts

Table of Contents

Table of Figures

Disclaimer

It's truly sad that we live in a world where I have to write this section, but my lawyer, my accountant and my colleagues have threatened to use various parts of my anatomy as bookends if I don't include it, so here it is.

The publisher and author make no representations or warranties with respect to the accuracy or completeness of the contents of this work, including, and without limitation, warranties of fitness for a particular purpose. No warranty may be created or suitable for every situation.

Nothing in this work is a promise or guarantee of earnings. The content, case studies and examples shared in this work should not be assumed to represent in any way "average" or "typical" results. Neither the author nor the publisher is familiar with you, your business, your market or your circumstances. Therefore the case studies we are sharing can neither represent nor guarantee the current or future experience of other past, current or future clients. Rather these case studies and examples represent what is possible by applying the strategies presented.

Each of these examples is the culmination of numerous factors, many of which we cannot control, including pricing, market conditions, product or service quality, offer, customer service, personal initiative, and countless other variables, tangible and intangible. Your level of success in attaining results is dependent on a number of factors, including your skill, knowledge, experience, ability, connections, dedication, focus, business savvy and financial

How To Get The Most Out Of This Book

1. Take Notes

This book and the related resources and guides, represent your opportunity to firmly establish yourself at the top of your field.

To get the maximum effect, read the book first then go to www.AuthorityExpertBook.com/register and sign in to download the resources you need.

2. Develop An Action Plan

In this book I set out the exact steps you need to follow to get your authority book ready and published in as little as 45 days. However, my experience is that unless you sit down and create a detailed plan of what you need to do, and schedule it in, your authority book is never going to make it out of your head and onto paper.

Once you've read through the book and decided what kind of book you're going to write, and how long you want to allow yourself to

Authority!

get it written and published, you need to create an action plan for yourself. You need to be clear what steps need to be done, when, and most importantly by whom, which brings us to the next topic.

3. Identify And Gather Your Resources

There is a reason why authors have traditionally worked with publishers, and that is because publishers have access to skills and resources that writers do not. As you read this book I will highlight the skills and resources you will need to get your book done. Think about who can provide you with that support. For example, you may need interviewers, interviewees, a ghostwriter, editors, designers, a marketer to launch your book, an email scheduling system, a web designer and webmaster, social media specialists. You may also want to work with someone to keep you on schedule, and you may want to collaborate with other experts as a co-author.

4. Get Clarity

If, after you finish this book, you still think all of this seems too confusing or too much like hard work then you may want to explore how my team and I could support you in getting your authority book written, published and in the hands of your potential clients. To find out more visit

www.robcuesta.com/tenthousandclub

Please note, we can only offer a handful of these sessions each month and demand is always higher than the number available, so there is an application process.

Introduction: The Ultimate Client Magnet

If you are reading this book then I am going to assume you opened it because you are a professional who wants to grow your business by attracting new clients. You may be well established, or just starting out. Either way, you are on your way to getting a huge advantage over your competitors.

In this book I am going to introduce you to one of the most powerful ways I know to get new business. It is a strategy that taps into some of humanity's most deeply ingrained cultural imperatives. It can position you at the top of your field in moments, and consign your competitors to the status of also-rans and nobodies.

When I tell you what it is, your immediate reaction may be "I can't possibly do that." You're not alone in thinking that – I'll be sharing some statistics to show you are in very good company. All I ask is that you bear with me, because in this book I'll be showing you that actually it is much simpler than people think to implement this strategy, and implement it with great success. And I'll show you how to do it in as little as 45 days if you truly want to.

It is a strategy my clients have used to get millions of dollars' worth of leads in a matter of weeks. A strategy that helped me close a $20,000 consulting deal in a few hours with someone who hadn't even heard of me until that morning. A strategy that can get you past any gatekeeper and bring you to the attention of your hottest targets – even if they've been ignoring your emails and not returning your calls for the last 3 years.

Imagine going to a sales meeting. As you are shown into the room you pass your competitor leaving the room, looking very pleased with how they have done. Inside, the executive you are meeting is still holding the business card and brochure your predecessor left, clearly impressed by what they heard.

You shake hands and open your case. "Before you start, I have something for you." You reach in and hand over something that focuses the meeting very clearly on you, and leaves your competitor... nowhere.

Right now, you are holding what I consider to be the trump card of business cards. The most powerful client magnet I know. A simple book.

It's a very specific type of book I call an 'authority book', because it is intended to establish your position as an authority in your field, a high-level expert worth paying attention to. And more importantly, faa high-level expert worth buying from.

I remember one of my favourite business experts, Peter Thomson, telling a wonderful story about meeting prospective clients. He had just published another book and decided to take copies with him to his sales meetings.

He opened his first meeting with "I thought you'd like a copy of my latest book." The prospect was delighted. "Would you sign it for me?" he asked, passing the book back, and a pen. Through the rest of the meeting he kept looking at the book, sneaking a peek at what was inside, like a child who has just found their Christmas present on top of their parent's wardrobe in the middle of October. Needless to say, Peter won a very lucrative consulting deal as a result of that strategy.

Or imagine getting a phone call from a company you've been trying to see for months, maybe even years. Or maybe someone you didn't know existed until that moment. "Hi. I've been reading your book. We need to talk."

Since ancient times, human cultures have (with a few unsavoury exceptions that preferred burning books to reading them) admired writers. Published authors are held in the highest regard, at the top of their profession. After all, they quite literally 'wrote the book...' And quite rightly so.

Writing a book gives you membership in a very exclusive club. There are seven BILLION people on Earth. According to the New York Times, 81% of Americans want to write a book—and I have no reason to assume that people in Canada, the UK, Australia and many other countries are far behind. And yet, each year only 2.2 MILLION books are published worldwide (according to statistics gathered by UNESCO).

That seems a lot of books, but it still means that if each book was written by a separate person – which it isn't – only 0.03% of the population actually writes a book. And since many of those books will be written by people who have already written a book before, the actual percentage is guaranteed to be MUCH lower; probably closer to 0.01%.

As I said: a VERY exclusive club. In fact, I call it The Ten Thousand Club. Why 'ten thousand'? 0.01% is 1 in 10,000.

Now, if 81% of the population want to write a book, but only 0.01% ever actually do, what happened to the other 80.99%? There are many reasons that stop intelligent people getting their thoughts out of their head and onto the printed page. Here are the most common ones I hear.

1. I don't know enough
2. You can't put what I know into a book
3. I can't write
4. I don't have the time
5. I'll never get a publisher
6. The firm won't allow it
7. Why would anyone read my book, when there are already hundreds of books on the subject written by people who are more well-known/more intelligent/more successful/more established/any other excuse you feel the need to cling on to

In this book I am going to systematically take each of your excuses away from you until you have no excuse for procrastinating. Then when I've done that I will show you how you can get your book written, edited and in the hands of the people who need to read it, all in 60 days or less.

Now, before we get started, let me share some observations and helpful notes.

Some Notes Before We Begin

A Note On Terminology

Now, before I go much further, it's worth pointing out that this book is written for you whether you are a consultant, coach, accountant, lawyer, dentist, doctor or any other kind of professional who charges for providing a service based on your knowledge, experience and expertise.

However, that's quite a mouthful to keep saying. So from this point on I'll use the terms "professional" or "expert" for the person and "expertise" or "advice" for what you do. Simply so we can keep this book under 500 pages long!

Also I haven't distinguished, except where it was absolutely necessary, between sole practitioners and firms with multiple partners and fee-earners.

So it doesn't matter whether you're a dentist practising on your own or a partner in a sizable consulting firm: the ideas in this book will apply to you.

Finally, remember one key distinction. The experts who read this book and fail are the ones who look at different ideas and think, "that would work for a coach (for example) but not for me because I'm (say) a lawyer." The experts who take this book and succeed will be the ones who read the examples and think "well that isn't my business, but how can I make it work in my industry?"

If you want to make these ideas work in your business, there is a way to make them work.

A Note On Grammar

As you read this book I would like you to imagine that I am having a personal conversation with you. This means that at times there will be instances that won't be grammatically correct, for instance I know it's supposed to be 'to whom you sell' not 'who you sell to', but I would never say it that way if we were having a conversation, it is just too formal. So whilst your old high school English teacher might have apoplexy at some of the things I've written, I hope you will understand why, and there is no need to email me about any grammar mistakes you find (don't laugh – it happens!).

A Note On Examples

Throughout the book I've given examples based on real life, both my own and my clients. The names and details that could identify their business have been changed simply because it would be hard to go back over 12 years of clients and ask them all for permission to quote them in the book. However, the key teaching point I wanted to illustrate remains.

A Note On QR Codes

You'll also find QR codes at various points. These appear next to web addresses, and if you scan them with a smartphone they will take you quickly to the page references.

And with that out of the way, let's look at what this book is about.

Enjoy the book.

Rob Cuesta
Oakville, Ontario, December 2014

What This Book Is, And What It Isn't

This is not a book for aspiring writers. I am not going to teach you how to build a career as a professional writer. More specifically, I am not going to teach you how to get rich from royalties on sales of your books. This is a book for business professionals who want to know how to use books to help grow their business.

What kinds of business does it work for? I wrote the book *primarily* for "professional experts": business consultants, accountants, lawyers, medical practitioners, wealth advisers, coaches... My favourite way to describe them is "anyone who makes their living by charging for the grey goo between their ears".[1]

---

[1]If your business does not fall into that category, take heart. I have seen this strategy work in all sorts of industries: hotels, restaurants, cleaning businesses, guest houses, building services, window repair and installation, car dealerships ... it can work in pretty much any industry.

Authority!

This is not a book about grammar or spelling, or indeed 'writing technique'. There are many books on those topics already. This is a book about how, in a short space of time, you can get your knowledge, experience and ideas out of your head, into a book, and listed by Amazon and other major booksellers.

This is not a book about writing fiction. This is a book about creating non-fiction books, guides and handbooks.

This is a book about turning you into *an author*, but not necessarily *a writer*. If you are already a writer, good for you. You'll be able to use what you learn in this book to write your book far more quickly than you might have thought possible.

And if you're not a writer, fear not. You'll be able to use what you learn in this book to *get your book written* far more quickly than you might have thought possible.

If you follow the advice in this book, you will be a business *author*. Whether you are a *writer* at the end of the process is totally optional, as we shall see.

About Me

Before I go much further, this is probably a good point to tell you about my own experience as a writer, publisher and—more importantly—owner of a busy and growing professional practice with clients across the globe.

As I write, I am looking at copies of my latest two books. Both were released in the space of 5 weeks. Both were #1 bestsellers in their categories on Amazon.

In total I've written 6 books under my own name since 2011, four of which were #1 bestsellers, and the other two were top-10 bestsellers. This book was one of those bestsellers, and reached #1 in 3 categories on Amazon within 10 hours of being released. That is not an accident. Like everything in business, there is a process and a system to make it happen.

I am not saying any of this to impress you. I am saying it as a backdrop to what I am about to write.

Growing up, I struggled with the English language.

My parents emigrated from Spain to England in the early 1960s, escaping brutal oppression at the hands of the Franco regime and crushing poverty. In the UK they took the only jobs they could: my father worked as a slaughterman in an abattoir, and my mother worked as a housekeeper in a hotel. By the time I was born they had learned English, but at home we spoke Spanish within the family.

So at the age of eight, when I went up to middle school, I was put into remedial classes for English. It was almost inevitable.

Of course, it didn't help that when the headmaster of my new school interviewed me and asked what we had done at my primary school, I replied "we *readed* and we *writed*..."

Oops!

Granted, in later years I turned down a place at Oxford because I felt it was 'too academic', graduated with the highest honours from another highly-rated UK university, joined one of the top professional services firms in the world, later joined their biggest competitor and then left to get an MBA with distinction at one of the highest-ranked business schools in Europe before starting my own consulting firm, but the fact remains: at one stage I could barely string two words of English together to make a coherent sentence, let alone write a book.

Interestingly, as I look back at the firms I worked for before setting out on my own, I realise that I had always known—unconsciously— that books were a critical way of establishing your place 'at the top table' in any profession.

I remember how, just after leaving PwC, I was in a local bookstore and felt a thrill of excitement when I found a book in the business section written by a partner at the firm. Naively, I didn't realise the true purpose of what I was holding.

A few years later, while I was at Deloitte we published a collection of short (30-60 page) books that were mailed to C-level executives of companies we were already working with and—more importantly—companies we wanted to work with.

That time I realised exactly why we were doing it.

And so, in 2003 when I struck out on my own and set up a fledgling consulting and coaching business, the first thing I should have done was to write a book. I didn't.

Why?

Because I didn't think I knew enough. I didn't think I could write (that scarred little 8-year old was still in there, kicking himself for the "readed and writed" mistake). I was far too busy trying to grow the business, and besides there were already hundreds of books written by people I thought were far more qualified, experienced and well-known than me.

The list may sound familiar (if not go back a couple of chapters, or more simply ask yourself why you haven't written an authority book yet).

Also, it was 2003 and there was an even bigger block in the way: the only way to get a book published back then was via a traditional publishing house. And publishing deals were rarer than unicorn's teeth[2]. The world today is a very different place for authors, as we shall see later in this book.

In fact, it wasn't until 2011 that I finally got round to writing something.

And I haven't looked back.

My clients include major global organisations like Microsoft, SAP, HSBC and State Street Bank. I have coached partners in 'Big-4' professional service firms on developing their personal brand. And I have helped hundreds of experts in small professional firms around the world to grow their businesses through my books, videos, presentations, workshops and mentoring programmes.

And with all that said, let's start by looking at why I use authority books in my own business, and why I recommend them to my clients.

---

[2] In case you're wondering, that is the 3rd variation of that sentence that I wrote. I'll spare you the alternatives!

Tapping Into A Better Class Of Client

One of my favourite reasons for using books in business development is that readers, on the whole, make better clients.

According to a 2007 research study by the US National Endowment For The Arts and the National Center for Educational Statistics, there is a direct correlation between reading and (among other things)

- ✓ Communication skills
- ✓ Salary level
- ✓ Career success
- ✓ Personal fulfillment

Aren't you glad you picked up this book, you brilliant, successful person, you?

When you think about it, it makes perfect sense.

The statistics on adult literacy make for depressing reading.

Let's look at the UK. According to research by the Department for Culture, Media and Sport in 2011, 35% of adults (including 42% of men) don't read for pleasure.

The US fares even worse, with 52% of adults not reading for pleasure according to the National Endowment for the Arts. This is *possibly* related to other research that found that 50% of American adults are unable to read anything beyond an 8th grade level book.

Canadians, it seems, are far more bookish, with research by the Department for Canadian Heritage finding that 87% of Canadians read for pleasure, and 54% reporting that they read virtually every day.

So who is doing the reading? Well it's not going to be the unintelligent, the illiterate, or people stuck in a low-grade job where they barely have time to eat and sleep, let alone read.

Readers are going to be people, on the whole, who are intelligent, well informed, open to new information, and reflective.

Now I don't know about you, but I would far rather work with clients like that rather than with ones who are unintelligent, uninformed, close-minded and prone to acting on impulse.

The fact that they choose to read also tells us something more about the clients you will get with your book.

Modern business has become a battle for attention. We live in a world where average attention spans are measured in seconds, not minutes. Information bombards our senses in sound bites, infographics and bullet-points. Answers to every question and every problem are at our fingertips or in our pocket. In such a world, the most valuable resource you can have is someone's focus on you and your business. Now, a book is not the only way to get someone's focus, but it is the single best way I know to get their focus <u>and maintain it</u>—just watch someone who is engrossed in reading and you'll see what I mean.

Once someone has your book in their hands, you have a direct feed into their brain.

These are people who would rather read a 60-page, 100-page, or even a 200-page book for the information they want.

These are people who are willing to give you what has arguably become the most expensive resource in the modern economy: their attention. And they are willing to give it to you in large amounts.

Someone who reads your book will watch your 90-minute DVD rather than a 30 second YouTube video; they will read your 10-page sales letter rather than demand you give them a 3-bullet point summary, and they will sit down with you for a proper sales meeting rather than a 'beauty parade' with you and half a dozen other hopefuls.

Better yet, intelligent people like to consider and evaluate and reflect on what they are reading. So now you have your message getting someone's full attention and serious consideration, for a considerable period of time. In commercial terms that is gold dust.

And the ones who won't read your book?

They will be impressed by the picture on the cover and the gold seal that says you are a best-selling author. "Ooh, look at the shiny object!"

Now you're glad you not only picked up this book, you also read it.

Another factor to consider: clients you attract through a book will typically spend more, remain more loyal for longer, and refer more business to you than other clients.

> Take the example of one of my own clients, Peter. His company's book helped them attract prospects who wanted long-term contracts worth hundreds of thousands of dollars each year. Before writing their book, a typical client was worth around $5,000 of orders a year, and needed to be chased for sales each year. That's quite a shift.

So a book will get you better clients, who are nicer to work with and likely to pay you more.

What *won't* a book do for you? That is what we will look at next.

You'll Never Get Rich From Book Sales

Many of my clients are horrified when I suggest—as I will suggest to you later in this book—that they give away copies of their book. Writers, even people who are only writers out of commercial necessity, seem to develop a fantasy that a fat royalty cheque is going to land on their doorstep any day now.

Let me burst that particular bubble for you.

In the US alone, upwards of 300,000 books are published each year. Globally, as I said before, 2.2 million new books see the light of day.

That's a lot of competition for your new book, and it doesn't even start to take into account the books that are already in print. According to publishing industry research firm R. R. Bowker, there were over 2.8 million titles in print in 2004 just in the US (and the number will be considerably higher now).

So how many books can you expect to sell?

Authority!

According to the New York Times in 2010, the average US non-fiction book sells fewer than 250 copies a year and fewer than 3,000 copies over its lifetime. Of 1,000 business books released in 2009, only 62 sold more than 5,000 copies.

Now, add to that the fact that for a niche non-fiction book royalties are in the order of $1 per copy and you can see why I'm suggesting you hold off from ordering the Aston Martin for now.

If you haven't picked up on it yet, I'll say it again, and I'll say it explicitly.

In this book I am going to teach you how to use a book to make money by using it to grow your business. I am not going to teach you how to sell millions of copies and retire to the Bahamas on your royalties.

Over the last few years I have given away hundreds of copies of my books, and I can attribute hundreds of thousands of dollars of income to those books. Some of that comes from product and service sales that have been influenced by my being a best-selling author-expert in my field; some comes from the level of rates that I command as a best-selling author-expert in my field; and some comes from the fact that it is much easier for people to refer me to others thanks to my status.

Now, don't get me wrong. I'm not saying you should never sell your book. All I'm saying is that if your intention is to monetise your book, most of that money will come from activities that require you to give your book away, as we will see in the chapter on Turning Your Books Into Bucks.

Your book is not a book. It is not a product. It is not an income stream for your business. It is a marketing asset. In fact it is a marketing asset that—depending on how forceful you want to be—either supplements or replaces your business card, brochures and catalogues, white papers and all the other paraphernalia you've been handing out to try and get a meeting.

With the right planning and execution, your book will open up new income streams for your business, allowing you to sell more products and services, acquire new clients or sell more to existing clients, and even create new products and services based on the book itself.

All of these are worth far more than a paltry $250 a year in royalties.

In 2012 at a conference I struck up a conversation with the person in the seat next to me. She asked me what I did and rather than launch into an elevator pitch I reached into my bag and gave her a copy of one of my books. As there was a speaker on stage I didn't say much, I just smiled and turned back towards the front. By the end of the conference she had read the book and signed up as a client in a $20,000 mentoring programme. At $1 a book commission I would have had to sell 20,000 books to match that conversation.

Some of the income streams we will examine in this book include

- Bigger, faster lead generation pipelines
- Higher win-rates on sales meetings and better conversion from sales letters and calls
- Speaking engagements
- Free publicity and PR

Authority!

- Better, higher-value referrals
- Better conversions from mail campaigns
- Free promotion of your business by other people
- Higher fees and prices thanks to a higher-end positioning in your market

Your task is simple: you need to get as many of these income streams flowing, as quickly as you can.

And if you have no idea how to do that, take heart: that is what this book is about.

Your Book Is Your Gate Keeper

How much time do you spend dealing with enquiries from people or organisations that are totally unsuitable to work with you? Perhaps they don't actually need what you are offering, perhaps they just aren't the kind of client you want to work with.

Worse still, how often do you start working with a new client only to realise somewhere down the line that you shouldn't be working together?

Your book can be a crucial way of applying what I call a Velvet Rope Policy, avoiding some of those wasteful and embarrassing situations, and saving you valuable time and resources.

Think of a swanky nightclub. You can always tell that a nightclub is swanky because they have a velvet rope strung between two brass posts and jealously guarded by a couple of security staff. Until that rope is pulled aside for you, you're not going in.

The rope and the security men are there for a very good reason: to make sure only the right people get in. And the reason for *that* is that if the wrong person gets into the club they probably aren't going to have a good time and they will probably stop the other patrons from enjoying the club too. If that happens too many times the club's reputation suffers.

Your business isn't all that different from one of those nightclubs. You have to let the right clients in and keep the wrong clients out in order to keep getting the right results and getting good testimonials and referrals.

Your book can become the velvet rope for your business through how it is written.

1. **You can explicitly say who should and shouldn't be reading the book.** That's exactly what I did in the opening of this book: "If you are reading this book…" I have also said several times that this isn't a book for authors who want to learn how to make a business out of selling copies of their book.

2. **You can show who you work with by association.** Talk about your past clients. Talk about who you enjoyed working with most, and why. Your readers will soon decide whether those are the kind of people or organisations that they identify with.

3. **Set out your criteria.** For example, I could be quite open here and say that unless a potential client has a marketing budget set aside so that we can do something useful with their book, we're probably not a good match. Why? Because there is nothing worse than having a client invest $5,000-

$20,000 or more in getting their book written and published and then they turn around and say they don't have any budget to use it in their marketing; they can't even afford to buy copies of the book for their key targets, for example. I know because it's happened.

4. **As you write, your personality will shine through.** The reader will figure out what kind of person you are, what is important to you about how you run your business and the clients you work with, and they'll be deciding whether or not they like you. They will love your ideas or hate them: either way the book is helping them choose.

5. You can even be quite prescriptive and just refuse outright to work with anyone unless they've read your book.

One of my favourite – and most successful clients was a referral. The company was a subsidiary of another, larger company. An executive in that company had been referred to me, and before calling he got a copy of my book Secrets of a Six-Figure Expert. His opening comment to me was "I loved the book and we need to make this company the Natural Expert at what we do."

Now, 'the Natural Expert' is a concept I created and explained in that book, so I knew before we started that he had read it and had bought into the ideas.

He arranged for me to meet the GM of the subsidiary and his management team. Before the meeting he told them all to read the book. As a result, the meeting wasn't about marketing; it was a meeting about how we could help their company become the Natural Experts in their field.

Authority!

Can you guess what I got that client to do, to establish themselves as the Natural Experts? We wrote a book. Then we ran a campaign of direct mailings built around the book: email, letters, 'lumpy' mail.

It was all made possible by the fact that they had a marketing budget in place for the year, and without it they wouldn't have got 6 leads worth almost $1 Million.

In case you're wondering, the Natural Expert is what I want you to become: the firm every client in your market wants to work with, over and above all your competitors, whatever it takes, and however much it costs.

So if you haven't yet written an authority book of your won, you need to. Which begs the question, "why haven't you?" That is the focus of the next chapter.

Why You Haven't Written A Book Yet (And Neither Have Your Competitors—But They Will After They Read This Chapter)

. . . .

As I said before, there are seven main excuses professionals come up with to explain why they can't write a book when I propose the idea to them.

1. I don't know enough
2. You can't put what I know into a book
3. I can't write
4. I don't have the time
5. I'll never get a publisher
6. The Firm won't allow it
7. Why would anyone read my book?

They are all exactly that: excuses. In this chapter I am going to take those excuses away and free you up to do what you need to do: write.

1. I Don't Know Enough

When I first start to talk to an expert about writing a book they typically fall into one of two camps.

The first camp believes that they don't have enough expertise to fill a whole book. The second camp feels that their knowledge is so expansive and encyclopaedic that it could never fit into a single book.

"I don't know enough" is the excuse of the first group—I'll come back to the second group in a moment.

We live in a world that can at times seem like it is flooded with information. We carry laptops, tablets and even phones that give us immediate access to the combined knowledge and experience of the entire human race.

So it's hardly surprising that sometimes we look at that world and we think "actually, I don't know that much."

To make matters worse, most professions and most firms encourage us to seek help when we are at the limits of our knowledge. It's essential for risk management. On a personal level, however, having to seek the advice and knowledge of other people who—by definition—are more knowledgeable than us (at least on the specific topic we are querying) again makes us feel like our knowledge is lacking.

And finally, human knowledge is growing and advancing faster than at any time in human history. Whatever field you are in, research and reflection are constantly adding to the pool of knowledge and we just don't have time to keep up. So by the time we finally get to read the latest professional journal, another two issues have been published and we feel as if we are falling even further behind.

If you've ever felt like that (and it happens to everyone, experienced practitioners as well as the newly qualified) let me share an exercise I do with my clients.

Imagine this line represents the continuum of all the knowledge in your field of specialisation. You can be as specific in defining that field as you want. If you are an expert on agricultural land reform laws in modern China, then that is what the line can represent.

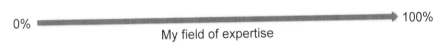

Figure 1: Your level of knowledge

The left-hand end of the line represents 0%. Total lack of knowledge. In fact, not even realising that your field exists.

The far right end of the line represents total knowledge. That end is, of course, unattainable, because every time you even think you are getting close, some so-and-so comes along and has a new idea.

Your personal level of knowledge, skill, experience—however you want to think of it—is somewhere on that line. I want you to put a mark on the line at the point that represents your personal level (if

Authority!

you're reading this as an ebook, draw the line on a piece of paper and do the exercise).

Now, look at that line and the mark you added. Wherever you put the line, there is a gap between the left hand end of the line and your mark. That gap represents all the people who know less about your field than you do. Or to put it another way: *all the people you can help*. These are the people who will learn something from your book; the people who will get value from what you know.

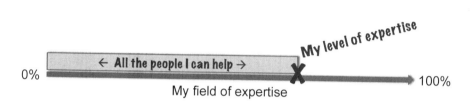

Figure 2: Who can you provide value to?

So the reality is, as long as your mark isn't on 'zero', there is value in getting what you know down on paper.

You also need to bear in mind that you probably know more than you realise. There's been a lot of research into how people learn. One of the key models of how we acquire new skills and knowledge is known as the Four Stages of Competence, originally created by Gordon Training International. The big picture is that we go from being 'Unconsciously Incompetent', where we don't even know that a particular piece of knowledge exists, so we don't realise we don't know it, through two other stages, to the point where we become 'Unconsciously Competent' where our knowledge has become so ingrained that we use it without thinking, so we no longer realise that we know something. Driving is a great example.

As a small child I had no idea that there was a special skill that adults possessed, called 'driving'. I was in Unconscious Incompetence.

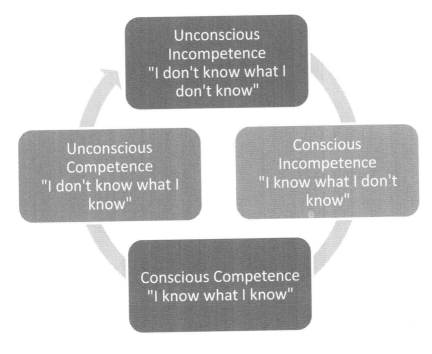

Figure 3: The Four Stages of Competence

Then at some stage I became aware that when we sat in the big metal box and went somewhere, my parents were sitting at the front, moving levers and turning wheels. They were doing something I had no idea how to do. I had moved into Conscious Incompetence.

As an adolescent I took driving lessons. At first there were checklists I ran through in my mind ("mirror, signal, manoeuvre" as I approached a junction); each time I saw a sign, I had to think what it meant and remember what to do about it. In other words, I knew how to drive, but I had to think about what I was doing; I had to concentrate. That was the stage called Conscious Competence.

Authority!

Finally, I reached a stage one day, without even realising it, when I didn't have to think about driving. Checking the mirror and signalling before I turned, had become an instinct. Interpreting road signs and reacting to them, had become a reflex. If you sat me in a car and said, "drive to work," I would do it without hesitation. But if you asked me to teach you *how* to drive, I would have had to sit and think about it first. More importantly I would have had to sit down and think about what you needed to know, and therefore what I knew. I was in Unconscious Competence.

So there are a lot of things about your field of expertise that you probably know without knowing you know(!). And it's that lack of awareness that can make us feel as though we don't know anything. Thankfully it's easy to put right by creating what I call an 'Interview With The Master' book, which we discuss in a later chapter.

> Another client that I loved working with is Philippa. When we started working together she had absolutely no idea how she was going to write a book. Indeed, she was convinced her knowledge wouldn't be enough to write an article, let alone a book. So I arranged for her to be interviewed by one of my team, an experienced business journalist and interviewer. At the end of the process it was as though blinkers had been removed. Philippa realised she actually knew a lot more than she had given herself credit for. Enough, in fact, for a book!

Still not convinced?

If you're still worrying about your credibility, then I'm going to suggest that you look closely at the section on creating a 'Panel of

Experts' book in the chapter "Introducing The Seven Authority Books". I'll explain more when we get there; just be reassured for now that worrying that you don't know as much as other people in your field can be an opportunity, not a weakness.

Now, the chances are that if you're reading this and you've been in practice for a while, your problem is not a lack of knowledge but rather knowing "too much". So let's look at the second doubt that stops experts from writing an authority book.

2. You Can't Put What I Know Into A Book

I get it. You're an expert. You know your stuff. You are a walking encyclopaedia of knowledge about your field. That's why you're in business: because you know 'stuff'. It's also why you could never write a book.

Because it couldn't do justice to what you know.

And because you wouldn't know where to start. Or stop.

And because it would take way too long to get it all done.

The key here is to filter.

First of all, accept that you can't get everything into a book. Or rather, you can't get everything *about every aspect of your field* into a book. The trick, if that's the right word, is to narrow down further.

For example, if you're a wealth adviser, don't try to write the ultimate guide to wealth planning. Instead, write a guide to using a specific type of investment as a wealth planning strategy, or a guide to making the most out of a single specific tax allowance.

If you're an accountant, don't try to write about every aspect of accounting: write about how entrepreneurs can maximise their write–offs against tax on, say, travel expenses.

The idea is to establish your expertise in one highly focused area, and then once you start to build a relationship with the reader (which we will discuss later in this book), you can introduce them to the other things you know about.

Second, realise that if your objective is to turn the book into clients, you don't *want* to get everything into a single book. The reason is very simple: it's like giving a thirsty man a hosepipe to drink from. Remember: you spent years learning what you know; you want to write a book that can be read—and understood—in a matter of hours at most. If you 'brain dump' everything you know into your book you'll end up overwhelming and confusing the reader. And there is one rule that you need to remember at all times in your marketing: *a confused mind doesn't buy.*

If you confuse your reader—if you try to give them everything you know in one shot—they will run away, because if you make them feel confused then in their mind they will label *you* as confusing, and potentially even confused. And why would they want to work with anyone who is either confusing, confused, or possibly both?

Third, this is your opportunity to do your reader a massive service. The chances are they have tried to figure out a solution on their own already. They have found the hosepipe for themselves. They even went as far as staring down the end to see what was coming. And then they put it down, scared of what they saw.

Your opportunity is to be the one that takes the masses of information they found—much of it conflicting, because it will have come from multiple sources—and cut through the noise, the conflict and the confusion. Give them the essentials. Give them just enough to realise that they need help and that you are the one to help them. If you do that you will earn their gratitude and their custom.

The same solution that worked for Phillipa, who didn't think she knew enough—being interviewed by a skilled interviewer—works just as well for experts who know 'too much'. An interviewer who knows what to look for _as a lay person wanting to discover more about what you know is_ the perfect partner to help you sort through and focus on what's important; simplify your knowledge down to the key messages; and turn all your expertise into the perfect authority book.

3. I Can't Write

Usually after I've helped a client come to the realisation that however much they know is the right amount, the next thing that comes out of their mouth is "but I can't write!"

There's a very common misconception that being an author requires you to be a writer.

Let me ask you a question: what is more important in an authority book, that it contains only your words, or that it contains only your ideas, expertise and experience?

Authority!

Ultimately it is the wisdom in the book that matters.

So start by letting go of the idea that you have to be a writer.

Allow me to let you in on one of the dirty little secrets of the publishing world. The books you buy at a bookseller frequently bear little or no resemblance to the manuscript the author submitted to the publisher. When a book goes through a publishing house it is subjected to numerous rounds of editing. Some of the editors are looking for grammar and spelling errors, it's true, but as we will see later, there are also armies of editors whose job is to make the book readable and to make sure the book flows and is well structured. And it's not like having an essay marked when you were at school. The editor doesn't put a cross and say, "rewrite this": they rewrite it the way they think it should be written.

The net result is that only 10-20% of most published books is what the author originally wrote (especially for new authors), and the underlying truth is that many authors are actually pretty bad writers, *but they have great ideas.*

So one way to get past the problem of not being a good writer is to hire an army of editors to polish up your manuscript. It's a perfectly acceptable way to do it, and one which I have used with my own clients.

There is an even easier way, however, and that is to get a ghostwriter, which also happens to address the next challenge on our list, so I'll discuss it there.

4. I Don't Have The Time

One of the biggest challenges we face as professionals in practice is lack of time. There is simply more than enough to do with serving the clients we have, supervising our staff and going out to get more clients. There isn't time to sit down and write every day.

As I sit here, writing this book myself, I am looking across at my bookshelf. On the shelf I can see books by Donald Trump, Richard Branson, Jack Welch, and many other successful, famous, and presumably *busy* people. And you have to wonder, if you can't find time to write a book running your business, how does Donald Trump find the time to write the <u>dozens</u> of books he has produced?

Now I don't know for a fact whether he uses a ghostwriter, but I do know that if I was Donald Trump that is exactly what I would do. I would get a writer to interview me, get all my great ideas out of my head and then turn them into a book. I know that's what I would do because I've done it for my own clients.

After all, it's only a step on from getting someone to interview you to help clarify your thoughts: take that interview, transcribe it and turn the notes and transcription into a book. Only you get a professional writer to do it rather than doing it yourself.

So again, if you feel that you don't have time, pay attention to the description of an Interview With The Master book in the chapter "Introducing The Seven Authority Books".

Another solution, which is closely related to the idea of the Interview With The Master book, is what I call a "Live" book, so you may also want to look at that section in the same chapter.

Both of these techniques—the Interview With The Master book and the Live book—will allow you to 'write' your book with only a few hours of direct input from you. We're not asking you to sit and write 90 minutes a day for the next three months. Just sit down for a few sessions over several days with an expert and then let them do the 'heavy lifting'. Can you find few days to get your book done? Of course you can.

5. I'll Never Get A Publisher

So, you've got past thinking you don't know enough, or you know too much. You've dealt with your lack of confidence in your writing ability. And you've found time to get your book done.

But who is going to publish your book? Why would one of the big publishers be interested in a partner in a small professional practice in your hometown?

A mainstream publisher is looking for books that are going to sell. That means the book has to have mass appeal. If you are writing a book on a specialist topic for a narrow niche the chances are that a mainstream publisher won't be interested. The numbers don't add up for them.

And it doesn't matter. In fact, getting a contract with a big publisher is probably the worst thing that could happen to you. Let me explain why.

You are writing this book to get clients. I'm going to assume that you want those clients sooner rather than later. A traditional publisher can tie you up in endless rounds of approval, concept tests, writing and rewriting, editing and a dozen other activities, and before you know it two years have passed and you still don't have a book.

Can you afford to wait for two years to get your clients? Will the ideas you write about today even be current in two years?

Fortunately, publishing houses have lost their stranglehold on the publishing world. These days it is possible for an individual to get their book into retail channels without a publisher in the middle.

Which is pretty irrelevant anyway for our purposes. Yes, it's nice if someone calls and says, "I picked up your book in Barnes & Noble (or Waterstones, or Chapters, or whatever your national bookstore chain is). Let's talk." But it's not essential. We are not going to wait for people to buy our book.

So don't worry about getting a publisher. Later in this book I'll show you what you need to do instead.

6. The Firm Won't Allow It

This objection has many variations:

- The firm/company won't allow it
- My professional association/code of conduct/regulations won't allow it
- My boss won't allow it
- My business partner won't allow it

Now, before I go much further, let me restate: I don't know you or your firm; I don't know your industry or your local laws and regulations. So this is a good time to think about whether you need to talk to your professional association or your employer. In other words: seek the advice of a qualified professional.

With that out of the way, here are my thoughts.

Many larger firms have strict controls in place over what their staff can and cannot publish. It's understandable, and it's also not a problem. I've worked with partners in major firms who were convinced they would not be allowed to do what I was telling them to do. You can. You just need to work with the compliance team or whoever it needs to be and make sure you meet their criteria. The rules aren't there to stop you publishing: they are there to stop you publishing *something you shouldn't be publishing*. So think of that team as your ally; they are there to make sure you publish something worthy of having the firm's logo and name on it.

Similarly, many professional associations have regulations in place designed to protect the reputation of the industry and to protect clients from shady practices. If your profession doesn't allow you to discuss specifics of client situations, then don't do it: talk about the techniques and technicalities. If your profession doesn't allow you to talk about anything that could be construed as 'advice', then share client experiences: look at Secrets of Their Success books in the chapter "Introducing The Seven Authority Books".

Also, consider the flip side: in some professions there are heavy restrictions on what you are allowed to do to market you business. There are typically far fewer restrictions on marketing a book, if any. So an authority book can provide you with the ideal vehicle to promote your business without promoting your business, if you see what I mean.

If a boss is the obstacle, then it is likely to be because they are worried either about potential damage to the brand or—more likely—that you will end up with a stronger brand than the firm. You need to sell him or her the idea that the book is going to be good for the organisation. After all, this is about getting clients, so it means revenue. Also, if you are positioned as an expert in your field, it can only do the firm good if your name is followed by 'partner at the such-and-such practice'. In an ideal world you retain ownership of the intellectual property (IP) rights, but if the book uses examples from the firm's clients, or uses the firm's IP then that may not be possible. At the very least, however, try to ensure that you will always be identified as the author of the book, even if you leave the firm. Again, you may want to get advice from a qualified IP lawyer.

A business partner blocking you is exactly the same as a boss, but with a far more personal stake. Approach it in the same way.

So there you are. Those are the main obstacles that experts find are keeping them from writing an authority book. By now you should see that they are not really obstacles, unless you allow them to be.

Let's get back to some positivity, and look at another key benefit of having an authority book with your name on.

Authority Books Open Doors

In an earlier chapter we saw how your authority book can help you to close the door on unsuitable clients. In this chapter I want to look at how your authority book can also help you to get suitable clients to open their doors to you. In the same way as your expert book will become your gatekeeper, it will also allow you to get past other people's gatekeepers. Let me show you how.

As a fully paid up, card-carrying member of the Ten Thousand Club you are endowed with an air of authority, an air of mystery. For you, I have no problem using the word 'awesome', because you deserve it[3].

---

[3] It is one of my pet bugbears that the word 'awesome', along with 'excellent', has been relegated to the rank of 'really good'. The Oxford Dictionary defines awesome as "extremely impressive or daunting; inspiring awe." In other words, watching the first rays of sunrise appear over the edge of the Grand Canyon and bathe the canyon walls in golden light, revealing millions of years of layered history is awesome. Watching a mare

Remember in the last chapter I mentioned that on my bookshelf I have books by Donald Trump, Richard Branson and Jack Welch. These senior and well-respected people know that a book is such a powerful statement of authority that they needed to have a book of their own. And having a book of *your* own puts you right there on the bookshelf next to Donald Trump, Richard Branson and Jack Welch. That's positioning. *That's* awesome!

Now, your target has a gatekeeper.

If they are an executive then they have someone whose job is to make sure that they are not interrupted by anything or anyone not worthy of their limited time. By anything or anyone, in other words, who is not awesome.

Alternatively, they may have to be their own gatekeeper: their unconscious mind is in control, filtering out anything that seems irrelevant or uninteresting and not worthy of their attention. Anything that is less than awesome.

And those gatekeepers are essential. Today more than ever we are bombarded with messages and interruptions. According to Fast Company Magazine, we see roughly 5,000 advertising messages

---

give birth to a foal, and seeing it rise immediately onto its legs and start to run around is awesome. Looking up at the night sky and reflecting on the fact that the stars you are seeing are so far away, and the light has been travelling for so long, that some of those stars may not even exist any longer is awesome. The dedication and depth of knowledge needed to complete an authority book, put your name on it, and get it out into the world makes you awesome. In contrast, a triple-decker burger slathered in hot sauce and topped with Monterey Jack and jalapenos is quite definitely NOT "awesome".

every day. According to Gallup, the typical manager gets to work for a whole 12 minutes and 18 seconds between interruptions. And researchers at Harvard and The London School of Economics found that 60% of CEO time was spent in meetings and 25% on phone calls.

No wonder gatekeepers are busy filtering.

Your potential clients will do whatever it takes to avoid your call, miss your email and skip your meeting request.

At home they are watching TV and an advert comes on. What happens? It's time to go make a coffee or start channel hopping. If the show is recorded on their PVR they'll skip to the end of the break.

Reading their morning paper, they barely notice full-page adverts, let alone a small ad in the corner of the page.

Driving home, the buttons on the steering wheel allow them to change channels away from an unwanted radio ad without even taking their eyes off the road.

Your potential clients will do whatever it takes to avoid your advertising.

The only way you can get past that is to give them a reason to want to see you, hear from you or better yet call you. And then you have to get them to act on that reason: you must turn 'want' into 'will'.

Getting them to do that is one of the hardest tasks you face as a professional. Ask Frank.

Michael is the General Manager at one of my clients. He had been trying to get a meeting with the CEO of a major target company for three years. He and his sales team had written, emailed, called. They had even tried door-stepping, turning up unannounced one day when they were "in the area".

For three years they were met with silence. Every attempt at contact went unanswered. At the end of his tether, Michael took my advice and sent the CEO a copy of the authority book we had just published for him. Within a week the phone rang. "I've just been discussing the book you sent us with my colleagues on the board. When can we meet?"

A book turns you from a brochure-wielding salesperson desperate to pitch into an author-expert, someone with a view and a solution. The point is that if you turn up with a brochure then you are there to sell. If you turn up with a book—your book—then you are sharing valuable insight and information. That's a very different positioning.

Books have inherent value. We are used to going to a bookshop or onto Amazon and... horror of horrors... *paying* for a book. When was the last time someone happily paid for your brochure?

Even if your company insists on charging for your catalogue, that doesn't mean your customers are actually happy to pay for it. It just means that there are a lot more people out there who aren't reading your marketing material but should be.

Having a book arrive at a target's office from Amazon is one of my favourite strategies—it's what I got Michael to do—and I'll revisit it in the chapter on 'How To Get Your Book Into The Right Hands'. But put yourself in the shoes of your prospect. Actually, first put yourself in the shoes of their gatekeeper.

The morning post arrives. There are dozens of leaflets, pamphlets, brochures, sales letters, a couple of catalogues, a DVD and a CD. And an Amazon box addressed to your boss. What would you do with that material? 80% of it will probably go straight in the trash. The DVD and CD? They might survive, but only if you recognise the company they're from and you know your boss is interested. But the Amazon box? Have you got the nerve to throw an Amazon package in the trash? I thought not. So you pass it on.

> Funny story. One of my clients got an email from a gatekeeper. "Many thanks for the copy of your book you sent to XXX [her boss]. This is not his area of responsibility, so I've passed the book to XXX [another director in the company] and she will be in touch shortly." Now, be honest: when was the last time a gatekeeper redirected your sales literature to the right executive because you'd sent it to the wrong person? And then wrote to let you know what she was doing!

OK, back to our scenario.

Now you're the boss. Your morning post is on your desk when you arrive. You can see the usual array of letters, leaflets and other assorted sales materials that your assistant has judged you might be interested in. But there's something different there. An Amazon box. Have you ordered something and forgotten? Has someone sent you a present? What do you look at first: the brochure from your printing company or what's in the Amazon box?

I thought so. As my old mathematics teacher used to say: Q.E.D.

The key here is that a book flies in under the radar. People know what a brochure is for. They know what a catalogue is for. They know what a sales letter is for. And a CD. And a DVD. They know they're all forms of marketing They even know that your website is marketing too.

But a book? Books are entertaining. Books are informative. Books are *valuable*.

Better yet, books offer an escape. They give us the opportunity to get away from the ceaseless barrage of interruptions and marketing messages.

Back in my days at Deloitte I often commuted by train between home and London. It was a three-hour train journey. Looking around the carriage on the way home you would always see certain activities going on.

Some people would be sleeping, weary after a day that had started 12 hours earlier. Some would be chatting to their neighbour. Some would be tapping manically at their laptop. And some would be reading.

There were three kinds of readers. There were the ones idly leafing through a newspaper or magazine to pass the time. The ones flicking through work papers, clearly bored, and annoyed that they were having to do this even after a long day in the office. And the ones sitting engrossed in a book. Everyone else seemed more interested in what was going on around them on the train than in whatever they were trying to do. But the book readers were in a world of their own, finally free from interruptions after the long day.

People who begrudge giving you 30 minutes for a sales meeting will gladly sit and read your book for an hour or two if it's well written—and I recommend you make your authority book something that can be read in an hour or two. No longer.

There's also something enduring about books. One of my prize possessions is a book from 1898, "Cassell's Book of Pastimes". I have had it since I was a small child (and no, it wasn't new!) and it was my constant companion through school holidays. It is also one of the oldest things I own, beaten only by a glass salt dish from the mid 1850s that belonged to my great-great grandmother (or possibly great-great-great, I lose track of just how great she was).

Over the years I have happily thrown away thousands of magazines and brochures. I've deleted countless PDFs from my hard drive. I've abandoned reports in airports and train stations. I've tossed away CDs and DVDs. Even so, I cannot bring myself to throw away books. Once I have no use for a book I take it to a library or a charity shop. Better yet, I give it to someone who I think would benefit from reading it. The only way it will end up in the trash is if it as damaged beyond repair. And I am not alone.

Very few people throw books away. Even books they will never read!

> In early 2014 I had just emigrated from the UK to Canada. A couple of weeks into my new life I was house hunting and rang a local realtor. We were going through the usual questions about what I was looking for, and what my budget was, what my status was, etc. and then the phone line went silent. For a moment I thought he had hung up.
>
> "Wait a minute," he said. "Did you say your name is Rob Cuesta?" "Yes." "The author?" "Err, I guess so." "Oh my god! I've been reading 'Secrets of a Six-Figure Expert'. A colleague gave me her copy and told me I **had** to read it."
>
> That's *global* positioning.

Books Give You KLT

You've probably heard that people only buy from someone they "know, like and trust". The challenge in sales is getting to spend enough time with someone for them to get to know, like and trust you.

When I was at Deloitte, certain partners would be allocated to key target clients. Their job was to build a relationship with executives at that company, spend time getting to know them and their organisation, and ultimately—it was to be hoped—close a deal. The pursuit could take years and never go anywhere.

I've coached partners at other Big-4 firms who had similar responsibilities.

The problem, of course, is getting enough time with the target on a regular enough basis that they feel like there is a meaningful relationship being built. Calling up every quarter to ask, "is there anything we can do for you?" just isn't going to cut it.

How different would that situation be, however, if you could sit on that executive's desk every day? Or if you could spend a few hours with them at their home one weekend? What if you could be really open with them, and tell them what really drives you, why you're in the business you're in, and why you care that they should fix their problem? What if you could talk to them about your greatest client successes, clients just like them?

That is exactly what your authority book does. It sits on their desk. It goes home with them at the weekend. It sets out your ideas, your philosophy, your case studies. And all in a format that is inherently compelling and persuasive. But why is that so important?

Authority!

Why Authority Matters

One of the exercises I like to do with participants in my workshops is a little thought experiment.

Imagine for a moment that you are at one of my events and I am on stage presenting. Suddenly a youth in a hoodie bursts in and shouts "everybody out of the room. Now!" What would you do?

You'd probably ignore him.[4]

Now imagine that instead the door bursts open but the person who runs in and shouts "everybody out of the room. Now!" is wearing a police uniform. Now what would you do?

---

[4] I tried this at an event in Ireland. One of the participants held up his hand and said, "well, I'm from Northern Ireland, and up there if a stranger bursts into a room and tells us to get out we dive under a table and then look to see if he's got a gun!" It pays to be sensitive to local conditions!

If you said you would do as they said you are mostly right. In actual fact, the chances are you would look at me as the presenter to see what I was doing.

Either way, why is your reaction different? Because the police uniform gives the intruder instant authority. And why would you look at me to see how I am reacting? Because as the presenter I am the biggest authority in the room.

Robert Cialdini is one of the world's foremost experts on persuasion. You could literally say he wrote the book on persuasion, in fact. And in "Influence. The Science of Persuasion" Cialdini identifies the key factors that lead someone to pay attention to your messages and act on them. One of the six factors he discusses is Authority.

Humans are programmed by society to respect authority figures and do what they tell us to do. Without that, society would quickly descend into anarchy.

Savvy marketers spotted this a long time ago. It's why toothpaste manufacturers get dentists to recommend their toothpaste, and drug manufacturers get doctors to recommend their pills. The aura of authority is so strong we will even accept recommendations from actors who admit they're not a doctor but they play a doctor on TV.

People used to assume—wrongly—that Hitler was able to get millions of people to do his bidding through fear. In the 1950s Yale psychology professor Stanley Milgram showed us that fear wasn't necessary to make humans do inhuman things, just the appearance of authority. In a series of disturbing experiments he was able to convince members of the public to apply electric shocks to another person even to the point where it appeared they might have killed them, as long as the person telling them to do it was wearing a white lab coat and carried an official looking clipboard. If you want to despair of human nature you can find footage from the original experiments on YouTube.

If you never want to look at a librarian or receptionist the same way ever again you'll also find footage of modern versions of the experiment. In one recording I watched, an attractive young woman in her early twenties has just 'zapped' the other person in the experiment (in reality a stooge who is only pretending to be electrocuted: the wires aren't connected to anything). "He's not moving," she says, totally deadpan. "What should I do?" The stern looking 'scientist' looks down at his clipboard. "The rules of the experiment are that if he doesn't respond you have to apply a shock." The girl seems to consider this for a moment, then with a shrug and a smile she presses the button. Zzzzzzzzapppppppp!

In fact, Milgram and the other researchers who have repeated his experiment in the decades since then all found the same result: 61-66% of participants are prepared to apply what they believe to be fatal voltages to a total stranger in the experiment.

Here's the awful truth about the power of authority: if neo-Nazis wanted to start death camps and were looking for executioners, all they would need is a white lab coat, a clipboard and a trip to the local temp agency.

Authority is a powerful force in human behaviour.

And the aim of your authority book is to put you on a par with the doctors and dentists making those TV recommendations. It puts

Authority!

you on a par with the cop telling people to leave the room. In fact, it puts you on a par with the seminar leader that everyone looks to for cues on what to do next.

If you want to be freed from the relentless push to "sell, sell, sell", the key is to publish at least one book on your topic. It will give you the clout to tell people what they should be doing, rather than asking them if they'd like to buy.

However, it only works if your book has value; if it passes on your knowledge and conveys your wisdom. Which raises an interesting question.

What is Wisdom?

Your authority book needs to have value for your prospective clients. That means that you need to give more than pure information in it. Why? Because information is cheap or even free. Information can be found for free with Google.

Many years ago, when I was a management consultant, I wrote a paper for a professional journal about turning Information into Data. It described how companies need to take all the raw details they are collecting and turn it into something they can use to help them make better decisions. It was a good idea, but very basic.

Almost 20 years later (and 20 years wiser) I stood in front of an audience of consultants and professional advisers and told them that they—and now I'm telling you too—need to turn all the information you have about your field of expertise and turn it into Wisdom.

How exactly do you do that?

It's by applying something I call The Knowledge Chain. In it's simplest terms, The Knowledge Chain says this.

Information + Retention = Knowledge

Knowledge + Application = Experience

Experience + Reflection = Insight

Insight + Connection = Wisdom

Figure 4: The Knowledge Chain

Think of it like this.

You've probably read hundreds, if not thousands of books. And you've attended countless workshops and training courses. And you've read thousands of journals and magazines. All of those gave you a LOT of **Information**. But 99% of it is useless, because you didn't retain it.

However, from each of those learning experiences there are some things—maybe 1 in 100—that you retained. Maybe it's because it was particularly relevant to you at that time—perhaps it helped you find a solution to a problem you were facing—or maybe it's because there was a captivating story attached that made it stick in your head. Whatever the reason, you remembered that information and it became part of your base of **Knowledge**.

Now, knowing something is not—by itself—enough either. Knowledge has very little value unless we take that knowledge and apply it.

It's the application of what you know that creates your **Experience**. And now we are getting into something that actually has value, because if you can talk to a client about your experience of applying what you know, there are lessons in that experience that they can learn from.

However, we can take that experience and make it even more valuable. We do that by reflecting on our experiences and gaining valuable **Insight** that we can share with our clients.

Up to this point what we had to share has been pretty generic. Millions of people probably have access to the same information as you. Even when we think an idea is novel, and perhaps protected by Intellectual Property Rights or other legal barriers, it quickly becomes 'common knowledge'.

And the chances are that if millions of people had access to that information, some of them retained the same information as you and applied it. And they probably had very similar experiences to yours. The details may have been different because of differences in the context and how they applied it, but overall their experience is likely to be broadly similar.

So there's nothing unique about what you know, and very little that's unique about your experience.

However, when you reflect on that experience and draw your own conclusions it is easy to come up with unique insights. And that's where you start to create real value for your clients.

There is another level that you can take this to, and that is by drawing together all the insights you have gained from your experiences and starting to make connections between them. That's the point at which you are able to create new models of how things work. That's the point at which you start to challenge existing notions. That's the point at which you gain true **Wisdom**.

And because you got that wisdom by making connections between the unique insights you had, which were themselves based on the unique *combination* of experiences that you have, you can be 100% certain that no-one else will have the same wisdom that you have.

That is where you create maximum value for your clients.

That is your Unique Selling Point; that elusive "USP" all the marketing books have had you searching for.

And that is what you must build your products and services and workshops and books around.

Conversations Equal Clients

One of the most powerful ideas I share with my clients is that marketing is ultimately just a series of conversations. Some of those conversations happen in person, some happen online, others happen over the phone. And others happen through the written word. However the conversation happens, every client you have ever had, and every client you ever will have, started with a conversation. By the same token, every growth problem I have encountered in the firms that approach me to work with them can be traced back to a problem with the conversations they are having.

Why are you reading this book? It's because you want to grow your business. I know that because I told you right on the front cover that this is a book about growing your business. We had a little mini-conversation and it got you to read this book.

So now I know that you want to grow your business. Let's think about *why* you want to grow your business.

Authority!

Is it because you don't have enough clients? Then I can tell you you're not having enough conversations. If you want more clients, start more conversations.

Is it because you have clients, but they're not paying you enough? Then your conversations aren't creating enough value for your clients.

The amount of money someone is willing to invest in you is determined by how much value they see in working with you. It's like this. Imagine I offered you a $100 bill. If I said "you can have this $100 bill for just $150" the chances are you'd tell me to get lost. Why? I haven't shown you enough value in exchange for your $150.

How much value would I have to show you before you accepted the deal and paid me $150? I'd have to be offering you more than $150. How much more will depend on your perception of the risk of the transaction, what return you demand on your investments, and a host of other conditions, so I can't put an exact figure on it, but I know I need to show you more value than I'm asking from you.

Which brings us neatly to a point that I want you to understand, retain and apply: if you're not making as much money as you'd like, you're not creating enough value for enough people. So if you want people to pay you more, you need to create more value in the conversations you have with them.

Do you want to grow your business because you've got clients but they are currently the wrong kind of client? Then stop having conversations with the wrong people. Say you're a financial adviser who wants to work with millionaires, but you keep getting blue-collar workers as clients who just want to protect the savings they have. I am pretty sure that if I looked through your appointments diary I would find very few millionaires listed, and a lot of blue-collar workers.

A couple of years ago I was approached by a consultant who wanted to raise the quality of clients she was working with. "I keep getting clients who have very little money so they can't afford to pay my full rates. I have to offer them discounts or payment plans, or we stop working together before they've got a result." I asked her where she was getting her clients. "From local networking groups and a barter group."

Who was at those networking groups? People who didn't have enough clients and were out prospecting. Who was in the barter group? People who had cash flow problems and needed to rely on barter to keep their business going. She left the barter group and changed the networking groups she was attending and it transformed her business. And her rates.

Are your clients asking you to do things for them that aren't really in your area of expertise, or things that you don't enjoy doing? Then stop having the wrong conversations with them. Stop having conversations about the stuff you don't want to be doing and start talking to them about the things you are great at and want to be doing.

Over the summer of 2014 I realised that my own business had moved in a direction I didn't want. We had ended up as a general internet marketing agency doing everything from search engine optimisation to website design to traffic generation. How had it happened? Because for 18 months that was what I had been writing about and that was what I had been talking to clients and prospects about. It was keeping me too busy to go out and do the things I love: helping clients to position themselves at the top of their field, raise their fees and sell to a better class of client.

So at the end of the summer I decided to focus on helping my clients in three areas: premium pricing, publishing authority books, and selling from the stage and face-to-face (I sum it up as a three step process: *Position – Create – Get Paid*). How did I make the switch? By publishing books on those topics.

"Premium!" was released in July 2014. It became an Amazon bestseller overnight. In September 2014 I contributed a section on selling from the stage to a collaborative book I was involved in, "There's Money In This Book". That too became an Amazon bestseller within days of its release. And of course this is the book on publishing. Watch out for a full book on selling in the near future. And watch the Amazon charts!

Of course, writing about the 'right' topics isn't enough. You need to write a 'good' book, so let's look at that next.

What Makes a Great Authority Book?

OK it's time to address the elephant in the room.

Let's face it, there are a lot of very bad books on Amazon these days. 99% of the Kindle catalogue is poorly written, badly thought out, and probably not particularly original.

Here's the thing though: just because other people are producing bad books doesn't mean you will. It's like driving. There are a lot of bad drivers. I mean shockingly bad drivers. Drivers who think lane markings are like the silver lines down the middle of a Scalectrix track: drive on the line, and every so often switch lines at random. Drivers who believe they can safely brake in 20 feet when they're hurtling down the highway at 60mph. Drivers who think other people should always give way to them.

Does that mean I have to drive like them? No, of course not. I don't have to drive like an idiot, and you don't have to write like one.

So what makes a good Authority Book?

I ask this often in workshops, and there's a fairly consistent set of answers. A good authority-building book

- Has good content
- Is factually accurate
- Tells a story/stories
- Is well written and edited
- Is based on experience
- Is well formatted and designed
- Positions you as the solution to the reader's problem
- Has a compelling title, strapline and cover
- Feels like it has been written just for you, the reader

Let's look at these in turn.

Good Content

You will have picked up by now that I am a strong believer in creating value for your audience. Good book content creates value in one or more of three ways.

Hope: It shows the reader that a solution is possible for a challenge or problem that they have been facing. This is not the same as actually giving them the solution—only showing them that there is hope.

One of my clients, James, has a great example of a 'hope' book. James's company provides the capability for their target clients to deal with sharp spikes in demand and unexpected disruptions to their ability to serve their own customers. The book was written as a series of short stories about clients dealing with different disasters, and by implication how the reader could deal with similar situations in their own business. In reality, of course, it was teaching potential customers when to buy James's products and services.

Respite: It provides relief from a challenge or problem that they have been facing. I call this 'giving them an aspirin'. Imagine a doctor is walking in the park and someone approaches them in obvious distress. "What's the matter?" they ask. "I have a terrible headache." Immediately they spring into diagnostic mode. "Have you had a change of diet?" "I don't know." "Are you under more stress than usual?" "I don't know. I just know my head hurts." "Did you sleep with your neck at an awkward angle?" "I DON'T KNOW! MY HEAD HURTS!" What's going on here? The person can't think about anything other than the headache. And until that headache is reduced they won't be able to do anything else, even if it could help them in the long term.

Readers are just the same. If they are deep in some issue that is causing them pain—physical, mental or financial—they don't want to think, and they can't think, about anything else. The pain dominates their attention. The only way you can get through to them is to give them something that will reduce the intensity of their pain—maybe even remove it completely—long enough for them to think.

Let me give you an example. Say you are an accountant who helps businesses get through an inspection by the tax authorities. Ultimately you want to be hired by those businesses, but a business owner looking for advice on what to do when the taxman comes a-calling has probably just received a letter announcing an impending

Authority!

audit and is looking for help, not a sales pitch. So your book might be "10 actions to take in preparation for a tax inspection". And of course #10 will be... to hire a qualified adviser, which is likely to be you since they have been implementing your other advice. The book doesn't tell them how to get through the inspection, only how to stop running around in a panic and start preparing. Get the idea?

Inspiration: There's a lot of value in seeing how other people have coped with situations similar to our own, so books full of success stories are very popular. If those success stories include clients of yours then it is guaranteed to bring you fresh leads.

Factually Accurate

Whatever you say in your book has to be factually accurate.

The challenge for us as writers is that facts and details are often boring, confusing and frequently irrelevant to the big picture. It's OK to change stories to protect the identity of people you write about, or edit and filter details to make things easier to follow, but **you cannot misrepresent** what is or was going on.

My rule of thumb is very simple. Whenever I have to adjust facts, I ask myself a simple question: *"if the reader knew the full story, would it cause them to make a different decision?"*

Or you can make the question even more personal: *"would you be ashamed to admit the changes you have made to someone who has just hired you on the strength of what you wrote?"*

If the answer is "yes", then you have a problem.

Tells A Story/Stories

Books tap into deep and ancient undercurrents in human culture.

Books are associated with stories, and humans are a race of storytellers. Our caveman ancestors sat around fires telling stories. Long before humans could write, they passed down knowledge and wisdom orally—and they used stories to make sure the wisdom stuck.

There is a lot of psychological research that shows that when we feel strong emotions at the same time as we are taking information in, we are far more likely to recall it later.

Now, it's hard to get emotional about a table of data points or a graph (unless it shows rising tax rates, say), but it IS easy to get emotional about a story.

So if you want to help your readers remember you, tell them your story. If you want to help them remember what you do, tell them stories about what you've done. If you want to help them remember your products and services, tell them stories about people using your products and services. Get the idea?

Is Well Written And Edited

Ultimately, your authority book is designed to enhance your credibility and reputation. In order to do that it needs to be written in good English (or whatever language you are writing in) and it absolutely needs to be edited.

Non-writers often assume editing is just about spotting spelling and grammar mistakes, and helping you to cut back if you are too wordy. As we will see later in this book, professional editors have a much broader remit. There are editors whose job is to make sure that your content flows and makes logical sense. Others check that it hangs together (simple things like, if you say "as I mentioned previously", they will go back and check that you did say it previously—it is all too easy as you draft your book to move sections or delete them and mess up your references). Others will check that you achieved whatever goal your book was intended to achieve.

All of which means that your editors are very much your partners in success.

Is Based On Experience

There are lots of books out there already based on academic theory, please don't add to them. Your authority book is your chance to show your experience, insights and wisdom. That, as we have already seen, is where you create value for your readers.

It is your unique experience and reflections and insights that make your book what it is. They are the true USP of your business. They are what will convince someone to hire you over and above your competitors.

Writing from the heart and from experience is critical if you want your book to hit home and bring you clients.

Is Well Formatted And Designed

I remember a few years ago picking up a marketing book in Borders (which already tells you something about how long ago this was!).

I have no idea how good the content was. Why? Because the book looked like it had been photocopied from a manuscript typed up on an old manual typewriter. It even had graphs that had been created with underscores and upper-case I's for the axes and + signs and o's for the data points.

It looked terrible. And I just couldn't get past the poor formatting and design to get to the content.

Designing and typesetting the interior of a book is a skilled task. Go and get a copy of my book Premium! (If you haven't got a copy yet you can get it at www.PremiumPricingBook.com)

Notice how the way the pages are laid out is consistent all the way through the book. Notice how different levels of heading are used, and the fact that headings are uniform across all the chapters. Look at how different fonts and font sizes are used to mark out different types of text (examples vs. content). All of this makes the book easier to read *and* increases the perceived professionalism of the book and therefore the writer.

Positions You As The Solution To The Reader's Problem

Your ultimate objective in writing an authority book is to get people to hire you or buy your products. That will only happen if they believe you are the solution to their problem. That means that simply cataloguing everything you know about a subject isn't enough. You've got to show them how that knowledge puts you in a position to help them.

One of the most powerful things you can do in your book is to give actual solutions. Many experts are afraid to give away too much. The reality, as we have already seen, is that the clients who need to work with you are the ones who don't want to try to do it themselves, the ones who are willing to pay to have someone else take the strain and effort out of solving their problem, and the ones who are happy to pay a premium for the reassurance that comes from having an expert take care of things.

Ultimately, your authority book is not a simple 'how to solve your problem' guide, it's a 'how to get us to help you solve your problem' guide.

Has A Compelling Title, Strapline And Cover

These three elements—the title, the strapline and the cover design—are among the worst executed elements of many authority books.

While it's not essential to get your book read, it is useful, as we will see in the chapter "Turn Your Books into Bucks", and it will lead to more enquiries. So how do you make sure your book gets read? The way it works is this.

The task of your cover is to get your book noticed. Whether a potential reader is scanning bookshelves in their local bookstore or scrolling through the results of an Amazon search, the chances are that it is the covers that will grab their attention before they even notice a title. So you need an eye-catching cover.

What makes a good cover? Here's a simple exercise you can do.

First, find a bookshop in the real world.

Shops tend to highlight stock that is moving and stock that makes the interior of the shop look good. Bookshops are exactly the same: the books that have been arranged so you can see them are the books a that are selling well and the books that have great covers. So, walk around and see which books the staff have turned around so that the cover is visible.

At the same time, notice which covers catch your own eye. What are you drawn to and why? What colours? What designs? How are the covers laid out? This will start to give you some insight into what works.

Once the cover has drawn the browser's eye, it is the task of the title to get them to want to know more. They have to be able to get that 'more' very quickly—almost instantly, in fact—so what that means in practice is that the title has to make them want to read the subtitle. That in turn means that you need a title that arouses curiosity.

Finally, the strapline or subtitle exists to make them want to read the contents of the book. That means that it has to tap into their needs and desires or their fears and uncertainties.

Hook Them With Your Title And Grab Them By The Strapline

Between them, the title and strapline need to give your potential reader all the information they need to decide whether the book is for them, and create enough intrigue to make them want to open it.

So what makes a good title and strapline?

1. Promise a benefit. Readers of non-fiction books are either looking for a solution to a problem or trying to achieve a goal. For example, as I write I can see a book that I picked up not long ago. Its title is 'Make Sure It's Deductible'. Now, in theory it could just as easily have been called 'A Guide to Tax Deductions For Small Businesses', but be honest: which would you rather read?

2. Be brief. Brevity in titles equals impact. For one thing, the shorter your title is, the bigger the typeface will be on the cover. A short title with a long strapline is a simple way of achieving conciseness wile also getting your point across. A great example is my own book 'Premium! How Experts Just Like You Are Charging Premium Rates For What They Know. And You Can Too!' A good rule of thumb is to keep the main title under 5 words: after that people will start to struggle to remember it and tell their friends.

3. Target your specific readers. If you can make your prospect feel like your book is written just for them, they are much more likely to pick it up and read it. For example, 'Make Sure It's Deductible' has a near-perfect strapline: 'Little-Known Tax Tips For Your Canadian Small Business'

4. Be specific. How many habits do highly-effective people have? Seven. You know because Steven Covey told you. How many hours can you get away with working in a week? Four, according to Tim Ferriss. When I said that the strapline for 'Make Sure It's Deductible' is near perfect it's because I would have added a number: as soon as you read the strapline you think, "how many tax tips are there in the book?"

5. Build curiosity. I picked up Keith Ferrazzi's great networking book 'Never Eat Alone' just because I wanted to know what he meant. I love the title of Remy Stern's "But Wait... There's More! Tighten Your Abs, Make Millions, and Learn How the $100 Billion Infomercial Industry Sold Us Everything but the Kitchen Sink' because it's just SO bizarre. And yet you know exactly what the book is going to be about.

One exercise you can do which has great value for anyone considering writing an authority book is to look at the Amazon bestseller charts, both for your own field and for others. When you do that, you'll quickly get a feel for what sells: what kinds of cover have grabbed people's attention? What sort of title and subtitle have made people want to buy?

Free Resource

I've put together a document with 29 templates for highly effective title and multiple examples of real books that use them. It's an invaluable resource to inspire you in creating the title for your own book. If you'd like a copy, simply visit www.AuthorityExpertBook.com/register and registering your copy of this book.

Feels Like It Has Been Written Just For You, The Reader

Your reader should feel as though every word has been written just for them. When you describe a fear your clients have, the reader should think, "I have that fear." When you talk about your clients' hopes, wants and needs, your reader should think, "that's how I feel too." Your clients and examples are the characters in your book, and just like a good novel, your book should make your reader identify with the characters.

Before I put pen to paper (whether literally or metaphorically—I'll describe my writing method later in this book), the first thing I do is to sit down and decide two key things:

1. Who I want to read the book.
2. What I want them to do as a result of reading it.

Your authority book is a marketing tool. Like any marketing tool, it has to be created and used intentionally. Ultimately the intent might be to sign up new clients for a product or service, to generate enquiries, to warm up a lead, or you may have some other end result in sight. Whatever it is, you need to be clear what that is before starting to write as it will guide your choices about the content and structure of the book.

The other aspect is having a reader in mind. If your book is promoting a specific product or service this should be easy: the reader you are writing for is the ideal client you would want buying that product or service. If the book is more general then things get harder, which is why I always urge my clients to focus their authority book as narrowly as possible.

For example, it would be tempting if you run a general legal practice to write an authority book that demonstrated your knowledge of consumer law, family law, probate, criminal law, employment law, property law, marine law and any other kind of law you can think of. But who would read that book? Probably only another lawyer. You would be far better producing several books on specific topics like fighting a speeding ticket, launching a class action, contesting a will, or whatever. Each of these appeals to a specific person— someone with the problem addressed by the book—and is far more likely to get you the result you want: an enquiry.

Knowing who is going to be reading your book and why, will allow you to choose the exact content you need, but more importantly will guide the style and level of your writing: if your book is targeted at CFOs of Fortune 100 companies it will probably be written very differently than it would be if the target reader is a high school student.

So now that we've seen what makes a 'good' authority book, what kinds of book can we write? Depending on how we write our book, we will appeal to a different reader, and also achieve different objectives. It's time to look at the seven styles of writing that you can adopt.

Introducing The Seven Authority Books

In this chapter I am going to take you through seven different styles of authority book.

1. The "Live" Book
2. The "Q&A" Book
3. The "Top Tips" Book
4. The "How To Use Us" Book
5. The "Panel of Experts" Book
6. The "Secrets of their Success" Book
7. The "Interview With The Master" Book

What style of authority book you choose will ultimately depend on many factors, but primarily it is down to five things.

- What you are trying to achieve
- Where you are in the development of your business
- Your current level of expertise or status in your field
- How much time you have to get your book done
- How involved you want to be in writing your book

Now, as I have made clear throughout this book, this is not a book about how to be a full-time writer. It is also not a book about writing technique. If you're reading this book I am going to assume that you are a professional who is busy running your business. For that reason, the techniques I discuss in this chapter are not about sitting down in front of a computer for a few months to write your book. My aim for you, as it is for my own clients, is that you will get your book written in the next 30-60 days. That requires some very non-standard approaches to writing!

As you read the following descriptions, imagine yourself using different approaches and start to focus in on which specific approaches appeal most to you.

Writing The "Live" Book

A "Live" book refers to taking a live performance of your content—a presentation, webinar, workshop, or whatever—and transcribing it into a book.

It is one of the fastest ways to get your book drafted, since you are typically taking recordings of something you have already done. As a result, many professionals start out with a Live book as their first attempt at an authority book.

However starting from a transcription of a live event is also one of the slowest ways to then turn your draft into a finished book, The reason for this discrepancy is simple: when we present we tend to speak very differently from how we write. Usually, it is not even the same as how we speak in conversation. The result is that transcriptions are neither formal nor conversational in tone.

Also, in a workshop situation it is easy to get sidetracked by audience members, and the smaller the audience the greater the risk of detours.

So you will find your transcript going in many different directions in the middle of what would otherwise be a chapter.

> **A cautionary tale**
>
> Early in 2014 a client asked us to turn recordings of two presentations she had given—over 5 hours of audio—into a book. When we went through the transcripts, eliminated repetition between the two events, and removed interruptions, questions and blind alleys, we realised there was actually less than 90 minutes of 'real' content; that's just 9,000 words (45 pages) even before the editors got to work.

Writing The "Q&A" Book

The Q&A book is one of the easiest books to write. The starting point for a Q&A book, as the name suggests, is questions: the questions you hear everyday from your clients and prospects ('frequently asked questions', or FAQs), and the questions you *wish* your clients and prospects would ask you ('should ask questions' or SAQs).

These questions are there for two purposes.

FAQs represent the objections you hear most often. Answering them in book form allows you, in effect, to pre-empt 80% of the objections you are likely to hear in a sales meeting. As we will see in the chapter Turn Your Books into Bucks, this makes your book an incredibly powerful sales tool.

For example, when it comes to writing a book, I am often asked 'will it take a long time to write a book' and 'don't I have to be a writer to write a book?' Hopefully you can see that I have answered these questions in this book (the answer to both is 'no', in case you still have any doubts!).

The SAQs represent the criteria a potential buyer should be using in choosing an expert in your field. Answering the SAQs, therefore, is your opportunity to teach your prospect how to hire you and why. You can use these answers to position yourself at the top of your field, and deposition your competitors.

A great example of this is what financial expert Robert T. Kiyosaki does in his book Rich Dad, Poor Dad, where he points out that while most people consider their home an asset, it is actually a giant liability for most people, since most people have a mortgage. That simple repositioning effectively makes the reader wary of any financial adviser who then tries to tell them that a home is an asset (which of course is exactly what 99.99% of financial advisers do).

I'm a big fan of the FAQ/SAQ formula, particularly when I'm working with a client who does not like to write.

One of the best ways to create the content for your Q&A book is to create slide deck with each question on a separate slide and then record yourself delivering the presentation. You can then get your recording transcribed, and it will give you the raw text for your book, but you can also take the recording and cut it up into individual recordings—one for each question you answered. That then gives you video that you can use for a podcast, for social media, for your YouTube channel, on your website, indeed anywhere and in any way you wish.

Marketing guru Mike Koenigs refers to this as the 10x10x4, because ten FAQs and ten SAQs can provide enough content for a reasonable book. (The '4' refers to four additional video segments that you need in order to use the videos of the questions on your site and on social media).

A variation on the FAQ/SAQ formula is a pure SAQ book. These consist solely of SAQs, as the name suggests, and is therefore intended purely to deposition your competitors and leave you as the only option. You can often spot this formula from the title or strapline of the book, which will be something like "7 Things Your Dentist Isn't Telling You About Oral Hygiene"

Writing The "Top Tips" Book

A 'Top Tips' book is another easy formula to implement. It is created in much the same way as a Q&A book—you can do it by recording yourself presenting the tips. Alternatively you may already have articles, blog posts, videos or other content that you can repurpose.

There are two main traps to watch out for when creating the Top Tips style of authority book.

1. Because you effectively sit down and ask yourself "what does my prospect need to know?" it is easy to become too inward focused and start a brain dump. Keep yourself focused on the

essentials, and always remember that this is really about getting the client.

2. It is also easy to create a very disjointed book if you are selecting random tips. Remember to give your tips a structure.

A great example of the Top Tips style of writing is my chapter on selling from the stage in There's Money In This Book. If you haven't got a copy yet then I have to recommend that you get it, especially if you make sales presentations or run seminars where you promote your products and services.

Free Resource

If you'd like a copy of my chapter on selling from the stage, simply visit www.AuthorityExpertBook.com/register and registering your copy of this book.

Writing The "How To Use Us" Book

One of the most powerful uses for your authority book is to educate your client on how to buy your products or hire your services.

We have already seen how a Q&A book can help you to do this. A 'How To Buy Us Book' is another great way to do this.

In this style of writing you present the reader with examples of how your product or service can help. It's not case studies: that's the 'Secrets of Their Success book, which we will look at next. These are little stories of typical situations.

Again, it is easy to repurpose this type of content for other uses, for example videos.

Writing The "Secrets Of Their Success" Book

Everyone loves to read inspiring stories of success, don't they? It's one of the key ways to develop your own capabilities. Especially if the person whose story they are reading is very similar to them.

A Secrets of Their Success book takes your clients' success stories and gathers them together in a book that illustrates the power of what you do, but also shows your prospects that people just like them are getting the results they aspire to.

So start by picking your most successful clients and ask if they would be open to sharing their story with other potential clients. Once ten or so have agreed you are ready for the next step.

The second step is to interview each of your clients in turn. Each interview will become a chapter in the book. It is, in effect, an extended testimonial with elements of a case study. In particular you are trying to highlight how the client's life was before they worked with you—the challenges they faced, the impact it was having on them, how they had tried before (obviously unsuccessfully) to solve their problem—what the experience of working with you was like, and how things are different for them now.

If you can get the interviews to happen on camera rather than just as a sound recording then this exercise will provide you with a great deal of footage of living testimonials that you can use on your website, on social media, even on a DVD to send to potential clients.

A Secrets of Their Success book also has another great benefit for your business. The stories tend to become not only inspirational, but also aspirational. Your readers look at the people in the book, identify with them, and then realise that they could just as easily be one of your success stories.

The risk in this kind of writing is maintaining a balance between showing results and telling your secrets. In some professions it's absolutely fine to say exactly what you did, if there is no way the client could do it themselves. Medical fields are a great example of this, so are complex litigation cases. In other professions, you have to weigh up the benefit of telling the reader what they need to do, fully expecting that they will still come to you to get it done, against the fact that some readers will take the knowledge you gave them and try to 'do it themselves'. That's fine: people who are likely to go away and try to do it themselves rarely make good clients. And sometimes they try, realise they can't do it themselves, and come to you for help anyway.

Writing The "Panel Of Experts" Book

The 'Panel of Experts' book is a great way to establish your reputation in a new field, or to take your existing reputation to the next level.

In a 'Panel of Experts' book you select a number of experts who are at a higher level in your field than you are and interview them. Those interviews can then be transcribed to make the book, and the recordings can be used as content for other purposes.

Now it's not always guaranteed that you will be able to get the experts you want to agree to be interviewed. Typically, it helps if you have an existing connection to the expert in question. So, you might approach people who trained you, people who have mentored you, more senior executives and partners within your own firm, etc.

A neat twist on the Panel of Experts book is to approach highly respected clients and prospects. For example, a mergers and acquisitions adviser might approach a few past major M&A clients, but also the chief financial officers of the six organisations he or she would most like to work with. It's hard to resist a request along the lines of "I'm writing a book on where the M&A field is headed, and I'm interviewing key industry figures for their view. Could you spare me an hour to be interviewed?" And of course once you're in the room with them you can use the opportunity to build rapport, establish a relationship, maybe even suggest a presentation. I've known experts leave this kind of interview with substantial deals.

Whoever you interview, the recordings of your interview provide great additional material to be repurposed for the web, social media, a podcast or whatever.

The big challenge with this approach comes from the fact that you are working with influencers and key industry insiders; people who are typically incredibly busy. As a result, your preparation is key. You need to turn up ready to go: have your questions prepared, and make sure the interviewee knows ahead of time how the session will go. You can't afford technical glitches on the day: have your technology charged and ready, and have a fallback in place if anything goes wrong.

For example, when one of our clients says they want to create a Panel of Experts book we spend time helping them create a briefing for the interviewee and an interview guide for whoever is doing the interviewing, and we provide technical support and coaching to make sure the interview goes smoothly.

Writing The "Interview With The Master" Book

In an 'Interview With The Master' book, the tables are turned on you, and you are the expert being interviewed. A skilled interviewer will not only help you to get your ideas out, they will keep you focused on the end goal, help you to filter your ideas down to the essentials your audience needs, and give structure to what could otherwise be a random conversation.

For that reason, I always discourage our clients from trying to run the interview themselves. While it can seem a good idea to get a friend, spouse or employee to interview you, it is too easy for that approach to give sub-standard results; that's why we prefer to have our clients interviewed by professionals with experience of this kind of work.

Having watched many experts start down this track and then get bogged down in the rewriting, I am going to add an extra piece of advice: let the interviewer ghost write the book for you. Resist the temptation to ask for the transcripts of the interview and try to do it yourself. You are too close to the content, and it is hard to cut down your own words. If you try to edit yourself, you will create a sub-standard book, and you will end up wasting precious time that could be spent getting and servicing clients, and delaying the completion of your book.

Getting Past The Roadblocks And The Dangers

So we have looked at seven different approaches to writing an authority book. You will have noticed a common thread to most of them: the interview. Unless you are an experienced writer, the easiest way to get a book ready quickly is to get a professional interviewer to interview you (or your interview subjects) and then have a professional writer turn the interview notes and recording into a well-structured, well-written, professional book that properly conveys your authority and expertise.

In the words of so many children's TV programmes when I was growing up: "kids, don't try this at home".

Back in 2013 I was approached by a sales expert who had written "a 40,000 word book" and wanted help "tidying it up to get it ready for publication". I passed it to one of our editors. Then an email came in from the client: he hadn't included the first chapter when he sent over the initial draft, and he was attaching it now. I forwarded that to the editor, who emailed me back in a panic.

The first part had been 60,000 words, not 40,000, and this new "first chapter" was 18,000 words long—enough to be a book in its own right. To make matters worse, the 78,000 words were unstructured and the writer turned out to be dyslexic. Impressive that he had overcome his challenge to write a book. Not so great for the editor.

Instead of days to edit, the book took almost two months, during which all three of us—the client, myself, and the editor—became increasingly frustrated. By the end—after taking out the repetitions and "detours", major rewrites, and restructuring the whole thing into a book—78,000 words had gone down to less than 25,000. It would have been a lot easier to start with an interview.

With that in mind, in the next chapter we will look at how to get the most out of your interviewer. For now, let's start by saying "let them do what they are best at".

Working With Your Interviewer

Your authority book is based on material drawn from experts in the field. Depending on the type of book you are creating, you may be that expert, or you may be approaching other people, as we have seen in this chapter.

So how do you get that information quickly and easily, while at the same time ensuring that you are getting everything we need to create a worthwhile book that will represent you and your brand at its best? And how do we then turn that information into a professional authority book that properly conveys your status and expertise?

The answer is to use a professional interviewer. A professional interviewer needs two key qualities.

The first is the ability to listen: these interviews are about the expert, not the interviewer. Their job is to probe and investigate. Like a detective, they will pick up on small hints and clues in something you say, and use that to take your mind off into the recesses where knowledge lurks, reminding you of things you thought you'd forgotten, and even shaping new reflections and insights as the interview process forces you to make connections you hadn't consciously noticed before.

The second is the ability to put themselves in the shoes of the reader. The role of your interviewer is to understand who your audience is—their age, what they do for a living, their level of income and education, what's important to them, their needs, wants and concerns, and much more—and then interview you as if they were that person, asking the questions that person would ask.

Typically, you'll generate about twelve pages an hour of book content. So a 120-page book will need about ten hours of interview time. As you can imagine, if you tried to do that in a single day you would go crazy (and hoarse!), so when we do this for our clients, we generally split the interviews over 4 or 5 days.

Before the interview, work with the interviewer to brainstorm the key questions they will ask, and plan out your answers in bullet point or mind map form. This will jog your memory before you start and prime you with the key points you want to discuss.

During the interview, the interviewer will work hard to get the best out of you. Their role is to

1. Keep you on track. As you work on each chapter, their task is to make sure that your answers are relevant to that chapter. If you start to head off on a tangent, they will gently guide you back to the matter in hand (or more forcefully, if you know that's what you need)

2. Push you if it seems like you haven't given enough attention to something that appears interesting. One of the challenges for you as an expert is that much of what you know is—to you at least—commonplace and mundane. However, to a layperson what you consider obvious and uninteresting may actually be a key insight

3. Get you unstuck. They will look through the book outline and your answer plans and prompt you

4. Ask you to bring what you are saying to life. Stories are a great way to back up what you're saying, so the interviewer will be looking for opportunities to get you to illustrate your point with war stories, personal anecdotes and examples

5. Make sure you enjoy the experience! Books must be informative and serious, of course; particularly authority books. But unless a reader is enjoying themselves, they won't keep reading. And if you didn't enjoy yourself while you were creating the content, that is going to come out, and they won't enjoy reading. So your interviewer is there to make sure the experience is fun and enjoyable.

Hopefully this has helped you to understand why it is so important to have an experienced interviewer. Otherwise, it is very easy for things to get out of hand and then editing becomes a much longer, and more expensive, task.

Getting Your Book Ready For Production

So you've planned your content, you've been interviewed, and the interview has been transcribed. What's left to get your book ready for production?

1. Get Your Manuscript Edited

The first task is editing. To people outside the publishing world, editing is all about looking for errors and cutting down the book to make it read better. These are important elements of the editing process but, as we have already seen, they are not the only ones. Editing actually covers five key areas

1. Correcting spelling and grammar mistakes
2. Making the book more readable by adding headings and subheadings. These help readers to understand the book at a glance, and also make it easier for them to find specific passages that they are looking for

3. Making the book hang together. This involves reading through the book and ensuring that where you refer to other parts of the book those parts are actually there (if you say 'earlier we discussed X' they will check that X came earlier in the book). The editor will also check that the structure of the book makes sense: is it ordered logically? Does it cover everything it needs to? Does the book make sense as a whole? And so on.

4. Making the book flow easily. The editor will add 'signposting language' to keep the reader engaged as you transition from one topic to another, from one chapter to another, or one section to another. Look in any well-written book and you will find things like "Now that we've discussed X, let's look at the next element, Y."

5. Making the book more engaging. This may involve rewriting entire passages, or removing them, asking for new passages to be added, or asking for ideas to be explained more.

These five tasks may be performed by a single editor, but are more often carried out by a team of editors, each focused on a different aspect of editing. Your relationship with your editor is one of the most critical relationships in the entire publishing process. The closest parallel would be the relationship between a patient and their cosmetic surgeon. Actually, I'll go further. It is like the relationship between a parent and *their child's* cosmetic surgeon. After all, the editing process is about taking your baby—your book— and making it beautiful.

Many authors try to edit their own book. This is fraught with dangers. Let's look at where those dangers are.

1. **Spelling and grammar mistakes:** Now some of these are honest mistakes. Sometimes your fingers slipped on the keys; sometimes you started to write one thing and then you went back and changed something, but the sentence ended up getting fragmented and hard to read; and sometimes autocorrect gets things a little wrong. Using a spellchecker doesn't always help, because it doesn't know that a word that is spelt write is actually the wrong word (go back and look at that sentence: my spellchecker says it is perfectly correct). Sometimes, though, you don't actually know that you've chosen the wrong word or that what you wrote isn't grammatically correct. And if it's you doing the editing, you aren't going to see anything wrong.

2. **Adding headings and subheadings:** Actually, there's nothing wrong with you doing this in principle. The challenge is that you know your book well, and you know your way around what you wrote, and so you may not see where a reader needs more help.

3. **Checking the book hangs together:** Again, your familiarity with the content will get in the way. You know what you wrote, but you may not always remember *where* you wrote it, or that you took it out after you wrote it, so you may not spot problems with the book's structure.

4. **Book flow:** This is an area that you can do yourself. Just make sure that you don't stick to the same one or two sentences: have a range of transitions in mind that you can use.

5. **Engagement and cutting:** This is the hardest for an author to do himself or herself. Every word on the page is there for a reason, otherwise you wouldn't have written it. Every

Authority!

anecdote and story is both essential and perfect. You see no reason to change a thing.

So, you drafted your book and now it has been edited. What's next?

Interior Design Isn't Just For Houses

In 'the old days' (before digital printing), someone would take your edited manuscript (Latin for *written by hand*), some plates and a rack full of metal type letters and 'set' the type in the plates—a process referred to as "typesetting". In our digital world, typesetting is still done, but these days a book designer takes your manuscript and makes design choices about the page layout, the fonts to be used for your body text, headings, sidebars, quotes, exercises and so on, how colours and shading will be used, and all the other aspects of designing your book.

At the same time your book receives some additional pages or sections, including

- the title page
- the preface
- the copyright/cataloguing page
- a dedication
- contents table, table of figures, etc.

The result is a book interior that looks professional and is ready to be printed.

The key is to create an interior that is

- **Consistent** in its use of fonts, weight and sizes. There's nothing worse than a book that uses twenty different fonts, all in different weights (bold, normal, extra bold, and so on). It looks jumbled and amateur—not words you want associated with your ideas.
- **Visually attractive.** You need your readers to keep reading. Bad choices of colour (or shade, in a black and white book) will make the book hard to read. So will bad choices of font or heading format, and many other design choices you might regret later. Similarly icons and shaded boxes to highlight different types of content (exercises, key points, stories, etc.) will make the book easier to read and more engaging.
- **Balanced** between text and 'white space'. There's nothing worse than reading a book that is too crowded. It makes the text hard to read. Similarly you don't want too have too much white space around the text or it will look like you don't have enough to say and you're just padding the book out.

Back It Up

The next stage of getting your book ready is to create the back cover blurb or 'copy'.

Think about what a reader does in a book store. They pick up a book because of it's cover. They want to know more because of the title and tagline. So what's next? They turn it over and read what's on the back. If they like it, they'll open the book to read more, but it's that blurb that draws them in.

Go to your own bookshelf and look at books on your own subject. Read the back cover copy and ask yourself "what made me buy this book once I'd picked it up?" What clues did the copy give you about what the book would be like? Did the blurb reflect the tone and style of the author?

Good back-cover copy is short and punchy. It appeals to the reader's self-interest, and answers the key question: "what's in it for me?" without giving away too much. And finally, it ends with a reason to buy the book.

There is one thing that the book blurb definitely isn't: a summary of the book. A summary gives everything away. Your blurb is there to build curiosity and desire. They're not the same.

It's A Cover-Up

Finally, a graphic designer creates an eye-catching cover for your book, so that it will stand out on bookshelves and in Amazon searches (or iBooks, Barnes and Noble, or wherever else it is being sold).

What makes a good cover? Here are some of the guidelines we adhere to—of course it would be almost impossible to apply all of the principles to a single cover, and there are always exceptions, but take a look at the covers of bestsellers on Amazon or in your local bookstore and you'll see many of these principles in use.

1. **A cover that 'pops'.** What does that mean? Even designers struggle with this, but in reality it means you need to play

with contrast. Look at movie posters: they often use teal and orange because it's a pleasing colour combination *and* the orange jumps out of the page. Dark colours on a light background achieve the same. I've received a lot of praise for the cover of "Premium! How Experts Just Like You Are Charging Premium Rates For What They Know And You Can Too!", which uses black and orange as the counterfoil to a green banknote.

Figure 5: A cover that "pops

2. **A simple central image that stands out** is very popular for non-fiction books. If you go for this *please* don't put it in a box: it looks amateur, especially if you combine it with a brown or beige background.

3. **A clever' or emotional image.** Non-fiction books in particular appeal to the brain, so images that catch *mental* attention work very well. Items that don't seem to belong together, or unexpected items, can work very well. They challenge us to try and "figure it out": e.g. Malcolm Gladwell's "Tipping Point" uses a single matchstick.

4. **Teaser text.** A tagline/subtitle or even an excerpt from a review can build interest without giving away too much

5. **An image of a person** on the cover can create instant connection with the reader, but it is difficult to pull off well for a non-fiction cover

6. **Text on its own** can work very well, and focuses the reader on the message.

One of the most valuable exercises you can do is simply to go down to your local bookstore with a camera-phone and take pictures of covers you love.

You can do the same exercise on Amazon. Back at your computer go through the images you've collected and ask yourself what it is that appeals. Is it the colours? The fonts? The images? How elements are arranged on the cover? Something else? Try and find the common elements across the covers you like.

Now compare this to the covers of best-selling books that you looked at earlier.

Take both of those exercises and when you combine the results what you have is the recipe for a potentially best-selling cover that you will love.

Free Resource

I've put together a collection of some of 20 of my favourite examples of effective book covers. To access the collection visit www.AuthorityExpertBook.com/register and register your copy of this book.

With all of these steps done, it's time for the book to go into production. But what do you do with the finished book? How do you get it in front of the people who need to see it? That's the topic of our next chapter.

Getting Your Book Into The Right Hands

So our book is in production. In the old model of the world we would now be in the hands of the gods. Or rather a publisher.

But the world of authority book publishing is different. From this point you are completely in control of your destiny. And completely in control of your profits.

The key is to make sure the people who you want to read your book get it. You can't afford to wait for them to possibly stumble upon it on Amazon: you've got to either drive them to the book or, better yet, get the book to them.

So in this chapter I will look at seven ways to do exactly that.

Give It Away

The most obvious way to get your book into someone's hands is to give it away to them. It seems a bizarre idea. You've invested time and money in getting your book ready, so why would you want to give it away?

So let's go back to an idea we've already explored. What is a client worth to you? If it's more than the $5-or-so that a copy of your book will cost you then it's worth giving away some copies of your book. And if you give away an electronic copy then it won't cost you a cent.

The key decisions you need to make are

1. Who are you going to give your book away to?
2. How will you get it to them?
3. What format will you give them?

The first question is easy to answer. You want to give your book away to people who fit the profile of your ideal client. Also, you want to give it to people who *know* people who fit the profile of your ideal client—ideally lots of them!

That means you need to start 'hanging out' where your ideal clients and their friends are, which is the answer to question 2, "how will you get it to them?"

You want to find what one former client of mine—David, a former Royal Marine and instructor in the Royal Air Force—referred to as "a target rich environment". That could be networking groups (although they aren't my favourite place to go looking for clients), conferences, Meetup groups, professional associations, or anywhere that your prospects gather in large numbers.

Emily has never sold a single copy of her book. Instead, she has given it away in response to the question "what do you do?" but only after chatting to the person to determine whether they would get value from it, and therefore would be a good prospect for her. That book has generated speaking engagements, consulting projects and workshops with large local accounting and law firms, and individual coaching clients. Before writing her book, she would charge clients $400, booking 3 sessions at a time. Her book has allowed her to book clients onto programmes for which she charges $2500 and more. All by giving away her book.

Which leaves the final question: should you give away a printed book or an ebook? My feeling on this is simple. The whole point of this exercise is to impress. A printed book that someone can hold and flick through screams 'expert' in a way that an ebook never will. So a physical book is preferable to an ebook.

However, there is a cost attached to giving away a printed book, and so you need to be selective. Ideally, you would only give your book to qualified leads, but that's not always possible. So in "Turn Your Books into Bucks" I'll discuss how to build a list of prospects by giving away your book on a website, and we will address the question of print vs. electrons in more depth.

For now, let's take away one key point: any time you find yourself talking to someone who is clearly a good prospect for your business, be ready to hand them a copy of your printed book. Free. Gratis. No charge.

The Brown Box

You're sitting at your desk one morning and your assistant brings in an Amazon box addressed to you. What do you do? You open it of course, and so will your prospects.

In an earlier chapter we discussed how sending a book in an Amazon box helps you to get past gatekeepers. But that's not the only reason why the Brown Box strategy is my favourite way to get a book into the hands of a key prospect.

Opening boxes from other people is a strong anchor for most of us. It feels like a birthday or Christmas (or whatever gift-giving holiday you prefer to celebrate). We can't help it. And for 99% of your prospects that is going to bring a bunch of positive emotions to mind, especially since Amazon allows you to gift wrap a book and send it.

So here is what you're going to do.

This is exactly the same strategy that got Michael a callback from a major corporation that had been refusing to take his calls or acknowledge his letters for three years. The same corporation that became a six-figure lead for him.

Write out a list of the top 50 people you would like to work with. Only include people whose name you know—not a title. In other words you are going to send your book to John Smith, not to The Director of Finance.

Next, get an address for each of those 50 people. It can be their office address, but if you know their home address that's even better.

Finally, sign up for Amazon Prime if you haven't already. Prime is an optional service provided by Amazon where, for a small annual fee, they will not charge for shipping on orders. You are going to be sending large numbers of books from Amazon, so it makes sense to sign up and save yourself the extra expense.

You are now ready to start prospecting. You or one of your staff members is going to log onto Amazon and start buying copies individually for each person on your list. You will have it gift wrapped by Amazon, and you'll include a gift card with a short message.

There are several different messages you can send. One is a request for feedback (which we'll discuss later in this chapter). Another way to approach it is to pick a section in your book that you think will be interesting or particularly relevant to the person you are sending it to, and add a note along the lines of "I've just released my new book. I thought you would be interested in the point I make on page 32. I'll call next week to get your thoughts."

That final sentence, that you are going to call later, is essential. Why? Because when you ring and the gatekeeper says "is she expecting your call?" you can legitimately answer, "Yes, I said I would call her this week".

The Personal Touch

The Personal Touch strategy is a development of the Brown Box designed to build curiosity and engagement. Instead of sending the book from Amazon, you are going to send the book from your office.

Start with a list of key prospects and their addresses, just as we did for the Brown Box strategy. However, this time get your assistant to write a Post-It note and stick it to the cover of each book as they wrap it up. The note should say something like "I loved this book, and I thought you would too. S" (or whatever *their* initial is).

Again, a gatekeeper is very unlikely to stop this book. The recipient is going to open their book and wonder "who is S?" Then they're going to think, "I wonder what they liked about it?" And then they're going to start reading. It's irresistible.

As long as your book has calls to action in it, as we discuss in the next chapter, you can look forward to some form of contact from your prospect.

I'd Love Your Feedback

The "I'd Love Your Feedback" Strategy relies on people's vanity for its effectiveness, which is usually a fairly safe bet.

You start, once again, with a list of key prospects. You can either send them a book via Amazon or you can post it yourself. Either way, gift wrapping is inappropriate for this.

In this strategy, the note that accompanies the book says something like "I've just released a book on X. As a leading figure in the field, I'd love your thoughts. I'll call you next week to discuss." And then your name.

So, what are we doing in this strategy? First, we are—of course—establishing our position as an authority on our topic. But then, by inviting the prospect's feedback, we are elevating their own status.

It's hard to refuse when someone asks us for our opinion, particularly if it is being sought because they see us as an expert or influencer. So you're unlikely to get a 'no' in response to this approach.

Again, a week after the mailing you ring up and ask to speak to them. And yes, your call is expected.

Help Me Write My Next Book

The Help Me Write My Next Book strategy takes the Feedback strategy to an even higher level. This time you are not contacting your prospect for feedback. You are asking them if they would agree to be interviewed for your next book as part of a Panel of Experts (which we discussed earlier).

As long as you already have a book, especially if it's a bestseller, and the book is relevant to your prospect, there are very few people who are going to say no. You can even include your earlier book as proof of your status.

And of course, the meeting is an excellent excuse to discuss what you do, and what you could do for them.

You're Selected

The final variant in sending your targets a copy of your book is to get your publisher to send the book on your behalf instead of you,

The recipient receives a book sent to them not by the author or a mysterious well-wisher, but by your publishing company. That already elevates your status well beyond anything else they could have received.

Along with the book is a letter explaining that they have been selected, as a leading figure in their field or community, to receive an early copy of this controversial/exciting/insert adjective of choice new book.

How you follow up is up to you.

Need some help?

If you'd like us to publish your book and, optionally, mail it out to your key targets visit www.RobCuesta.com/TenThousandClub

---

Make Your Book Available In As Many Formats And Shops As Possible

So far I have focused on writing a printed book, and different ways of giving it away. Now let's turn to some ideas for not giving your book away.

First of all, aim to get your printed book into the key online bookstores. Amazon is the 500-pound gorilla in its field, and you need to get your book listed there if nowhere else. That in itself will open you up to a global audience. The next obvious online sales site is Barnes & Noble, particularly if you are in the US.

Both of those sites will give you very high quality links back to your website if you set them up properly, which will help with your ranking on search engines like Google.

Notice that I haven't said anything about physical bookstores. The reality is, most people search for books and buy them online these days. Getting your book into a physical store involves additional expense and work that is unlikely to be justified by the likely benefit.

So where else is there to have your book listed?

The key is to make your book available in two other formats: ebook and audiobook.

According to Amazon, more than half of its book sales are now ebooks. That's a compelling reason to make your book available as an ebook. Again, the leader of the pack is Amazon's Kindle platform, with some industry observers estimating its ebook revenues at up to $520 Million each year, but don't ignore Barnes & Noble's Nook, Apple's iBooks (which will get your book listed in the iTunes store, an online shop-front with 8 Billion active buyers across virtually all demographics), and the multi-format stores like BooksAMillion.com.

The ebook version of your book makes your book accessible instantly to millions of potential buyers around the globe, including in countries where your print book may be hard to get hold of. Authors who publish with us automatically get their book in Kindle format, and we can additionally distribute to Nook and iTunes.

The final format you need to consider is an audiobook. Many people now like to listen to their book rather than reading, and this trend is likely to increase as use of smartphones, tablets and even media-aware vehicles continues to rise.

Authority!

In the world of audiobooks, Audible.com is king, owned—as you might suspect—by Amazon.

Creating an audiobook is not simply a matter of sitting down at your computer and reading your book out. For audiobooks, especially ones intended to increase your credibility, sound quality is critical. That's why we prefer to help our clients to create audiobook versions of their work using professional voice artists with experience of audiobook work.

So now that you have your book where it needs to be, let's see how you can use the book to make money.

Turn Your Books into Bucks

Admit it, this is the part of the book you've been waiting for. You want to know how a book is going to bring in more clients, and if possible allow you to raise your fees.

If you've been paying attention so far, it should not be a shock that most of the techniques in this section involve giving your book away. As I have said several times in this book, you are not here to get rich on royalties: you are here to get your book into the hands of as many of your ideal target clients as possible and convert them into buyers. So let's see how an authority book can help you get more enquiries, close more deals, and sell for more.

> Tom is an expert who until late 2013 had been working just with local businesses. In the space of under 6 months he positioned himself as an expert in helping businesses in a specialised medical field. He is now a regular speaker at international conferences and has been approached by national governments to help them expand their medical sector.

By now it should come as no surprise that it all started with a book. A conference organiser found it on Amazon and invited Tom to speak at their next event. Tom then built on that by releasing another book on the specialised field he was being asked to speak on.

Warm Up A Cold Call

One of the most thankless tasks you or your staff will ever face in selling is cold calling. Picking up the phone to speak to a stranger who has never heard of you opens you up to rejection, embarrassment, anger and a host of other reactions that—as human beings—we generally try to avoid.

Most books on selling aren't much help when it comes to dealing with this: reminders that "it's a numbers game" and "every 'no' brings you one step closer to a 'yes'" really don't do much to make the task any easier, or any more rewarding.

The problem is that everyone is guarding against cold callers: gatekeepers, business owners, executives, even consumers sitting down to eat. And I have to confess, I gave up being polite to cold callers long ago: as soon as it becomes apparent that I've just been interrupted by an unsolicited sales call, I don't even bother to say goodbye—I just hang up. And if they call back I hang up again without even saying a word.

So what is the modern professional to do in the face of that kind of resistance? It all comes down to positioning. Let's face it; very few people want to talk to a salesperson. And I know you're thinking "but I'm not a salesperson, I'm a..." whatever your profession is. But the problem is that in other people's eyes, if you are selling something you're a salesperson.

The solution is obvious when you put it in those terms: you have to position yourself as anything other than a sales person. How about approaching them as a best-selling author and expert in your field. Would that change things?

Books are a quick, simple way to reposition yourself. Think about it: how would you react to each of these approaches?

- "Hi, I sent you a brochure about our wealth planning services last week and I wondered if you have a few minutes to discuss it?"
- "Hi, I sent you a copy of my book 'Save It: Protecting Your Assets After Retirement' last week, and I wondered if you have a few minutes to discuss it?"
- "Hi, I'm calling from Peter Smith's office. We sent you a copy of Peter's bestselling book 'Save It: Protecting Your Assets After Retirement' last week, and Peter asked me to call and see if you would be willing to spend a few minutes giving him your feedback on it. Do you have your diary available?"

Expert-Authors get a far warmer reception than sales people do. Period. Your authority book will open doors that have until now been closed firmly in your face.

Remember the story of Michael from earlier in this book. Michael and his sales team had spent years door-stepping potential customers in their offices. Smaller companies had sometimes placed small orders, but larger companies had typically just refused to meet with them. Their main target had spent three years carefully avoiding contact, refusing to return calls or emails.

Mailing his authority book to target customers generated 30 warm sales meetings with smaller potential clients, and six major leads, including a call back from the big corporation that had been avoiding them for three years.

That's the power of using an authority book to warm up a sales call.

Higher Win-Rates On Sales Meetings

Let's face it; many sales meetings are awkward at best. Often your prospect is listening carefully, but only so that they can spot when to drop in one of the big objections they've already planned out in their head. And the colder the lead was originally, the more they are looking for an excuse to cut you off.

Having a sales meeting with a prospect who has read your book is an altogether different affair.

A lot of time is spent in sales meetings introducing yourself, establishing credentials, going over the basics of what you do and your product or service, and either pre-empting objections or dealing with them once they come out. Not so when your prospect has already read your book.

As the meeting starts, the person who invited you to come in to talk will introduce you to other people in the meeting. Normally that introduction sounds to the others like 'this is Peter Smith from So and So Ltd. I've asked him here to tell us about something he's trying to sell us."

When your host has been warmed up with a book the introduction is more likely to sound like "This is Lucy Smith. I read a copy of her book 'Productivity: How To Cut Your Down Time by 50%' last week and it filled me with ideas, so I rang Lucy and asked if she would come in and talk to us some more about it. Thank you for making time to come and speak to us, Lucy."

So already the meeting is off to a very different start. And if your host has made their team read the book in preparation for the meeting, so much better.

Next, think about handling objections. Normally in a meeting, as I said, there's a cat and mouse game as you try to head-off objections and your hosts try to cut you off with them.

One of the smartest things you can do in writing your authority book is to pre-empt the most common objections inside your book. If you do a good job of that, then most of the time when someone raises an objection your response can be "well, you may remember we dealt with that in chapter nine...". Of course a lot of the time the objection won't even get raised, because it's already been dealt with in the book.

One of my clients summed it up beautifully to me. "When I'm in a sales meeting now," he told me, "I let the book do the selling. Everything I used to spend time explaining in a sales meeting is in the book. All I'm doing is reminding them where. And it's a great feeling holding up my book and saying 'look here. That's the answer to your question.'"

Get Speaking Engagements

As a practicing professional I'm sure you go to lots of evening meetings, professional development events and networking groups.

When an invitation to a 'do' arrives, which is more likely to make you want to attend:

- "Mike Edwards, Sales Manager at So-and-So Ltd will be giving a 30-minute sales talk on employment law"
- "Best-selling author Mike Edwards will give a 30-minute talk 'Hired Can't Be Fired: 20 Expensive Mistakes Hiring Managers Make That Will Saddle You With a Nightmare Employee' "

I know which one is more likely to get me to go.

Event organisers are always looking for speakers for their events, and they need to find speakers who are going to be entertaining, provide valuable content for the audience, and get—as they say in the UK—bums on seats. It's far easier for an event organiser to sell a talk by an author than a pitch by a local professional or a sales rep.

Better yet, being the author of a bestselling book will get you invited to speak to bodies that are normally difficult to get in front of: professional associations, conferences, and so on. Organisers of these kinds of events guard their audience as jealously as a gatekeeper guards their executive. Their big fear is that you will come along and do a sales pitch.

Of course, the challenge with these events is that it's often difficult to gather contact details from the audience, let alone make a sale.

However, very few event organisers will say "no" if you offer to give a free copy of your book to anyone who attends, and it's perfectly reasonable to ask where to send that book to.

You need to make it as easy as possible for people to give you their details there and then. Now, it can be tempting to just add a slide at the end of your presentation and say, "If you'd like this, just send your name and email to this email address". There are two big problems with this approach.

First, nine times out of ten the email address you give will be either your own or that of your assistant. So you are now setting yourself or one of your staff up to have to follow up manually with people. That's great if you've given a talk to an audience of ten, but what if you spoke to 300 people? Do you really want to be emailing each of them back individually, or calling them?

Second, if you do it at the end of your talk, people just want to get up and go to the restroom or the coffee stand or the bar. If it is also the end of the event, they just want to get back to their car and out of the car park before everyone else. So they make a note of the email address—which they may copy down incorrectly in their haste—and promise themselves they will email you "later".

Now, if there is one thing I've learned in 23 years as a professional adviser, it's that 'later', more often than not, means 'never'. Once they leave the presentation, the real world starts to intrude. Inertia sets in. The paper where they noted your details gets lost. Emails and calls from their staff and customers drive all thought of your presentation from their memory.

So you need to get them to act right away and you need to follow up automatically. One of the tools we create for all our clients is what's called a Crowd Grabber. This is effectively a lead-capture page on a single side of paper. The sheet tells people how to claim their free book and any other bonuses you want to offer. They can email their details in or text their details to a special number.

Now, the chances are that 90% of the audience have their mobile phone with them: let's face it, very few people allow their phone to be more than 10 feet away from them at any time. So you can actually talk them through the sign up during your presentation: "I promised your organiser that I would give you a free copy of my book. Let me tell you how to get it. Who has a mobile phone with them? Great. Take it out of your pocket. On the sheet you've just been given, you'll see a telephone number. Start a new text message to that number. In the message box write your name and email address and hit send. You'll find your copy of the book in your inbox before I even finish my talk today."

I've known events where the sign up rate was more than 100% of the audience. How is that possible? Because people in the audience shared the Crowd Grabber with colleagues who weren't even in the room at the event.

The key is to have the contact details added to an automatic follow-up system which sends out the ebook of your book without you having to do anything.

A 2007 study by researchers at MIT found that when you follow up within 5 minutes of an enquiry, that enquiry is 22 times more likely to turn into a sale than if you leave the follow up for later.

If you try to do your follow-up manually the chances are it won't get done for a day or two, if at all. That's why we connect our clients to an automated system which includes options for communicating with people by email, voicemail and text, all on autopilot.

So, use your status as an author to get speaking engagements, then use your book (printed or the electronic version) as an ethical bribe to get people onto your list.

Turn Your Book Into A Seminar

Speaking at other people's events can be a great way to get leads and clients. However, speaking at your own events can be even more powerful.

These can be face-to-face events, in a meeting room, or virtual events by livecast, phone or webinar. They can be to a small, select audience, or you can fill a room with 100 people or more. You can be the only speaker, or you can have other experts—from your own firm or from other, complementary service providers, also speaking alongside you.

However you decide to do it, your book will give you the raw materials to write your seminar, and the credibility to get people into the seminar.

One of the questions I get asked most frequently about setting up seminars is whether they should be paid or free events. Ultimately, whether or not you can charge, and if you do charge, how much, depends on your market and audience. My preference is always to have a paid event, although I have been known to give tickets to those events as a bonus to people buying my products.

If you make your seminar a paid event you have the added advantage that—subject to any regulations controlling paid referrals in your profession—you can offer other people a fee if they send someone to your event. I will often give affiliate commissions of 75% or higher for those events, since my objective is not to make money from the tickets, but rather from the sales during the event.

As I mentioned earlier, I wrote a chapter in 'There's Money In This Book' on the key mistakes speakers make when they are selling during a presentation.

Free Resource

If you'd like a copy of my chapter on selling from the stage, visit www.AuthorityExpertBook.com/register and registering your copy of this book.

Turn Your Book Into Products Or Services

Your book can form the basis of a range of products and services.

The most obvious would be to provide implementation of the advice and techniques you discuss. For example, we offer a publishing service for experts like you, based on everything you are reading about in this book—I'll tell you about it later.

The next obvious product is a multimedia version of the content of your book. The written word is there to give your words gravitas, however many people find it easier to learn from audio and video.

Creating an online product, or a physical (CD and DVD) product based on your book will make your ideas more accessible for those people.

Next, think about what people do after they have followed your advice. Perhaps the ideas in your book provide the basics, or get someone through the first steps. If that is the case then you have an opportunity to create a product or service that takes them through the next step. Using my own business as an example again, the next step logically for some of the clients we have published is to create a sales seminar based on the book so you can sell your products and services on the back of it. To that end, one of the services we offer is a full-day Power Day where we sit down together and design an end-to-end sales presentation, and then I coach you on how to deliver it for maximum conversions.

Another possibility is to turn your ideas into a mentoring programme where your clients join you in person or online on a regular basis—weekly, monthly, quarterly: the choice is yours—to learn and implement your system and ideas. You'll need to supplement the meetings with online resources such as emails and webinars, physical elements such as newsletters, DVDs, CDs, and some one-on-one work.

If you have turned your book into a seminar, or you deliver other live events and presentations, recordings of your events will make great content for CDs and DVDs.

There are many other types of product (in my seminars I identify 68 different types of information product), but these examples should be enough to get you thinking for now.

Authority!

A key resource I can direct you to is the final section of 'Premium! How Experts Just Like You Are Charging Premium Fees For What They Know And You Can Too'. In it, I discuss premium business models including membership programmes, high-end products and one-on-one advisory work. If you haven't yet got a copy you can get it at www.PremiumPricingBook.com.

Build A List Of Potential Clients

One of the most valuable assets you can build in your business is an engaged list of potential clients.

The mistake 90% of professional firms make is that they do not gather the contact details of people who are interested in their products or services. Of the 10% that do gather those details, 9% then fail to engage with those potential buyers and waste the list that they have built.

Even if you never get as far as publishing your own authority book, please take one thing from the time you have invested in reading this far: *you need to build a list of potential clients, and you need to keep them engaged.*

Here are some statistics that should help to convince you of the importance of building a list.

50% of the people who visit your website will leave within 8 seconds. That's roughly the time it will take you to read this paragraph.

Why do they leave? Because there's nothing on the site to hold their attention.

Here's an even more troublesome statistic: on average, 99% of visitors to a website will leave without buying anything. What that means is that if you're paying to send traffic to your website, your costs to attract a customer are actually 100 times higher than you think they are. Say you're paying Google $5 for every click on a Pay Per Click advert: only one in every hundred of the people who click on your ad will actually buy, so it actually cost you $500 to get that buyer there.

Now ask yourself, "did the other 99 leave because they weren't interested?" It would be tempting (and lazy) to assume that the answer is yes. The reality is, some of them *did* leave because they weren't interested. They may have got to your site and realised that your product or service wasn't actually what they were looking for.

However, some of them will have left because they weren't sure whether your product or service was what they were looking for: if they reached your site and realised they were going to have to explore to find answers, or if the information you gave them was too confusing, or too superficial, or too complex, then they will click away.

Others will have left because the phone rang, or an email arrived, or someone knocked at their door, or the kids called out for them, or who knows what may have happened.

The point is this: *someone who leaves your site empty handed might still be a potential client.* But only if you can follow up with them. And for that you need their contact details.

Put those two statistics together and what you get is this: you need something that is going to grab someone's attention within 8 seconds of them arriving at your website, and will make them want to give you their contact details before they go.

Now, most attempts to build a list on a website consist of a box at the bottom of the home page that says "Sign up here for our newsletter". A newsletter is about the least engaging offer you can make in exchange for someone's contact details. When a visitor to your website reads "sign up for our newsletter", what their brain sees is "give us your email address and we will send you a bunch of random articles every week that you have no time to read, which is just as well because most of them are irrelevant to you anyway".

Back in 2013, I had just been engaged by a new client. In our first session together they told me that one of their big problems was that hardly anyone was opting in to their list. Their Google Adwords consultant was suggesting they spend more money on Adwords: if they were getting one person signing up each week with what they were spending, then if they spent ten times as much, they should logically get ten times as many people opting in. I told them to hold off from doing anything until I had a chance to look at their site.

Sure enough, when I looked their only offer was a newsletter. The reason for the low optins wasn't a lack of traffic. It was a lack of a decent reason for people to opt in.

So, what could you give away that is going to grab attention, and promise enough value for someone to willingly give you their contact details?

A book is the perfect 'ethical bribe'. Sending a printed copy is also a great excuse for requesting a mailing address, which will then allow you to follow up with a prospect by mail as well as by email. In a world where inboxes are dominated by spam, physical mailing addresses suddenly have real value again.

It is up to you whether you give away the book to anyone who asks for it (in exchange for their email address and possible their mailing address), or whether you get them to answer some qualifying questions first. You can even decide whether to send them a printed copy or an electronic version based on their answers.

You can create books targeted at very narrow groups of clients and use them to segment your list. The narrow appeal will also ensure that the people who order it are better prospects: 'A Guide To Fighting Your Speeding Ticket' may get thousands of requests, but if you're a law firm based in Toronto, 'A Guide To Fighting Your Speeding Ticket In Toronto' will help you to avoid having to post copies of your book to people in Alabama who will never be your client!

Once someone is on your list, your task is to follow up with them and engage with them until they either buy or decide they don't need you. But that is the topic of another book, not this one.

For an example of building a list with a book, visit www.AuthorityExpertBook.com/register. You'll see the kind of page you need to create for your own book.

Now, clients sometimes ask me why they can't just offer a free report or a consultation rather than a book, so let's look at that next.

Bigger, Faster Lead Generation Pipelines

An authority book will improve the quality of your lead generation pipeline. In the last chapter we looked at how to get your book into the hands of the right people, and in the last section I suggested using it as a bribe to build a list of potential clients.

Traditionally, professional firms have offered free reports or free consultations to encourage people to get in touch. The problem is, people know that both of those are going to lead to a sales pitch. Even if yours doesn't, a visitor to your website or a reader of your advert doesn't know that: they see 'call now for a free consultation' and alarm bells start to go off in their head.

Books don't trigger the same reaction. And if they have to pay for the book—either for the book itself or just for shipping—they will be even more off their guard.

A book also gives you multiple opportunities to invite them to take action: they can request additional resources or access supporting materials. By the time they have read your book they are likely to be more receptive to the idea of a free consultation because you have established your authority and already provided massive amounts of value, so getting them to call and ask for a meeting is far easier once they've read your book. It may take them longer to get there, but you'll have many more people taking you up on the offer.

Combine that with what I said right at the start of this book about the kind of people who are going to read your book, and you'll see how an authority book improves the quality of your pipeline in a way that a report of free consultation on its own never will.

Monetise Your Social Media

Many professionals tell me that they are mystified by social media; they just don't see how Twitter, Facebook, Google+, or even LinkedIn can help them make money.

> Back in 2011 I launched a new service. I started with 253 people I selected from my contacts on Facebook and LinkedIn. I told them about a book I had just written, which I offered them for free if they joined my mailing list. I grew that mailing list further by posting adverts about the book on Facebook and LinkedIn. Within 6 months I'd created over $90,000 of revenue from the list that started with that book.

Here's how you monetise social media: you run targeted adverts that promote something your audience wants—your book—and you give them the book in exchange for joining your list. Once they're on your list you are well on your way to turning them into a paying customer, as we saw.

Build A List Of Buyers

So far I've spoken a lot about giving your book away. I'm not totally against the idea of selling your book, however. After all, if you're reading this the chances are you bought this book.

The reality is, I have written books that were designed to be given away for the purposes of lead generation, and I have written books that were designed to be sold (but can still be given away, to the right prospect).

Buyers of your book are excellent prospects. In fact, I am going to correct myself. Buyers of your book are not prospects. They are clients of your firm. It doesn't matter that they have paid $10, or $20, or even possibly 99c for the Kindle version of your book: they have paid to get advice from you, and that automatically makes them more valuable than someone who has expressed interest but has never paid for anything from you.

The challenge is this: when you give your book to a potential client, you know exactly who they are and how to get in touch with them. When someone buys your book they are actually an excellent prospect, but there's no way to get Amazon or Barnes & Noble or whoever sold them the book to give you their contact details. You need a way to convince the reader to give you their contact details themselves. You need what we call 'an ethical bribe'.

The answer is to put multiple opportunities in the book for readers to take action, as we have already discussed. Those calls to action can take many forms.

- **Offer Boxes:** Offer Boxes (also referred to as Johnson Boxes) are sections of text that stand out because they have a frame, tinted background or some other formatting that marks them out from the surrounding text. In the offer box you can tell the reader about a resource, product or service—paid or free—that is directly related to what they have just read.

- **Inline Offers:** an offer box is a very direct and overt way to make an offer. If you prefer not to be quite so 'in your face' you can just insert the offer into your text, without giving it any special formatting. The disadvantage of this approach is that it is easy for the reader to miss it if they are skimming, and hard for them to find if they remember later that you made an offer but can't remember exactly where.

- **Links to an online quiz or assessment:** Cosmopolitan sells millions of magazines every month, and virtually every issue includes some form of quiz or assessment. People love to discover more about themselves or some aspect of their life, and so a quiz—free or paid—is a very compelling offer. More importantly for your business, the answers prospects give to your quiz can provide valuable insights that can help you qualify the lead and help you segment your list

- **Links to videos:** They say a picture paints a thousand words. Video has 25 pictures every second, so a minute of video is worth 1,500,000 words. OK I'm kidding. But video does have immense value. You can use video to illustrate concepts that are hard to put into words, show your readers what your clients are saying about the ideas you discuss, demonstrate the effectiveness of your product or service: the possibilities are endless. For the viewer, video offers the promise of a quick way to get more depth on what you are writing about.

So videos to accompany your book are a great supporting resource to offer in exchange for contract details.

- **Links to MP3 of related content:** In a similar vein, an audio to accompany a section of your book can be an appealing way to give more depth, your reader can put it on their MP3 player and listen in the car, at the gym, or on their commute. If you created your book from an interview you may already have a lot of audio material you could use as an 'ethical bribe'.

- **Links to downloadable tools and worksheets:** A great way to get someone to give you their details is to offer them tools and worksheets that help them to implement the ideas in your book. If your information helps people to save money then you could give away a calculator that works out how much they will save. If your information involves following a process, you can give away a planning tool. Use your imagination.

Whatever ethical bribes you decide to offer, you need a way for people to submit their details in order to claim their resources. The simplest way is to send them to a webpage. However, as we have previously discussed, it's always best to get people to act immediately, and your readers may not always have access to the web when they are reading your book. That's why I like to give multiple options for opting in. In this book you will see opportunities to not only visit a webpage but also send in an email, send an SMS or leave a voicemail.

As part of the launch of the book I also offered buyers of the book bonuses if they emailed in their receipt (you can see the bonus page at www.AuthorityExpertBook.com.

All of these different ways of opting in are powered by Instant Customer, the same tool I use with my clients.

Find Out More

You can find out more about Instant Customer at http://www1.instantcustomer.com/cmd.php?af=robc

Free Publicity And PR

If you've ever tried to get a press release or a story into the media then it will not come as any surprise to you when I say that journalists aren't interested in promoting your business for free. The launch of a new product or service is rarely seen as newsworthy by your local business journalist. They receive thousands of press releases and 'news' stories every day, so when you email to say you've just released a new product to the market it's just more of the same, and you'll probably be referred to their paid advertising sales team.

You need a story to tell. Journalists are looking for human interest. They are looking for something out of the ordinary; something that will make their readers take notice.

A local business professional who has released a new book, especially if it's a number one bestseller, is big news in most communities. An industry insider who has written a book is big news in most professions and industries. So you can use your book as the hook to get you into the media.

What you need to do is to choose your media carefully. What does your target client read, watch or listen to? And where will you find them in the highest concentrations?

Yes, your audience reads a daily paper, but their attention is as diluted as the paper's focus. If you get a slot in an industry journal targeted at your ideal client, their attention will be highly focused.

Ironically, the broader the audience, the harder it is to get into the media, and yet the less value it has for you. TV, radio, newspapers, magazines: they are all the same. In a general interest media channel your item will probably be little more than 'noise' for 99% of the audeince. You need to be more strategic in your choice.

If you are trying to break into a local market or grow your local presence then it makes sense to target local media: the local paper, community magazines, local radio stations, the local chamber of commerce and local business improvement agencies. Otherwise, look further afield.

Do you belong to any associations that publish a magazine? They might well be interested in your story. Examples might be your university alumni association, alumni groups for your past employers, industry associations.

You can also get your book reviewed to build up awareness. Contact the industry bodies and professional associations that your target clients belong to. Contact the training organisations that your target clients belong to. Approach the industry news sites they follow. Ask yourself: who is in regular communication with the people I want to sell to? And then ask those organisations and people whether they would like a copy of your book to review.

However you want to get into the media, and whichever media outlets you want to approach, the basic process is the same.

1. List the key influencers you want to approach. Get their names and mailing address
2. **Get a strong hook.** This may be the same as the general hook or your book, but it is likely to be different: your media hook has to be something that is going to appeal to the journalist and their audience, so each approach you make will be unique.
3. **Have a media kit on your website.** This will include a 'one pager' that tells journalists what you do and who for, photographs, recordings of past interviews, past press clippings. When a journalist comes to your site and finds a media kit ready for them it positions you as someone professional who knows how to deal with the media and will therefore be easy for them to work with.

Getting into the media is much easier as an author than as a business owner, but once you get into the media you become an insider: the next time a journalist needs an expert to interview for their opinion, you will be at the front of the line.

One of my clients is a local expert who made a choice to focus on working with clients in her local area. Her book got her a nomination for a national award for Influential Women. That got her interviewed by a podcaster, which in turn led to interviews on radio. Her big challenge now? What to do with the enquiries she has started to get from potential clients across the globe.

Free Promotion Of Your Business By Other People

Just as most journalists are too busy doing their job (reporting the news) to promote you for free, most other business owners are too busy doing their own job (growing their business) to promote you for free.

Getting them to tell their audience about something that will be useful to them is much easier. So you can treat industry podcasters and bloggers as another media outlet. Approach them in exactly the same way I outlined in the last section.

Your book can also help you to build joint ventures with other companies. Look around you. You probably know many other businesses and professionals who are working with your ideal target client and who aren't your competitor. The question is how can you convince them to tell their clients about you? You actually face a triple challenge

1. You have to get them to know, like and trust you.
2. You have to help them understand what you do.
3. You have to make it easy for them to refer you to their clients.

Your authority book makes it easy to do all three.

Say you are an employment lawyer and you want to set up a relationship with a local accounting firm. Or a chiropractor wanting to work with the local health supplements store. Or perhaps you are an insurance broker, wanting to work with a mortgage broker, or the local wedding chapel, or a car dealership...

You can approach the other party with your sales hat on or you can approach them with your author hat on.

When you approach them with your author hat on, as you hopefully remember from earlier in the book, their sales filter is down, so they are more likely to want to get to know you, it's easier to like you and they will trust you more easily.

The book will help them to understand your business and what you do.

And if you offer them a copy of your book for each of their clients (or at least the ones who would be good prospects for you), you make it easy for them to make the referral, as we will see in the next section.

You can offer them a box of books they can send out—they don't even need to give you anyone's name and address (you don't need it: you have calls to action in your book that will get the recipients to give you their contact details themselves).

You can offer books that they can give to attendees at their own seminars and events.

And remember, if you have written your book by interviewing other people, you have a list of people who now have a reason to give copies of your book away to their own contacts: they are the stars!

Better, Higher-Value Referrals

I'm sure you would love to get more referrals. As long as you train your clients to refer properly, referred prospects are great for your business for many reasons.

First, they tend to come **ready to buy**. Whoever referred them to you will have convinced them they need to work with you, and may have answered many of the questions they would have had. As a result they come with fewer objections and fewer challenges. You will still have to sell—a new buyer is a new buyer, whether they come by referral or walk in off the street—but it will be an easier, and far more comfortable sale than selling to someone cold.

Second, referred clients are **hardly ever shopping around**. When someone is referred to you by a friend they are generally only speaking to you, not comparing prices and packages with your competitors. Also, because they have been referred by someone they know, like and trust, some of that knowing, liking and trusting is automatically transferred to you. As a result they are typically less price resistant.

Third, referred clients are **far more likely to refer you** to their own friends and contacts. After all, the reason they are working with you is because someone referred them, so they understand the value of referrals, and they will even do it without you asking.

Fourth, referred clients often **spend more and are more loyal over time** than clients you generate for yourself. Even better, the person who referred you is likely to be more loyal to you as well: they convinced their friend to work with you, so it becomes harder to step away.

So why is it so hard to get good referrals?

Most professionals know they should be asking for referrals. Some even think their business is referral based, but aren't doing anything more sophisticated than sitting and hoping that someone is going to refer them.

I know, because for many years I was that professional: "I get most of my clients by word of mouth" actually meant that sometimes I was fortunate enough to have someone tell their friend about me. But let me ask you this: if word of mouth is your main way of getting new business, shouldn't it have a process? After all, that makes it a key business growth system. Would you run your business without a process for hiring new staff? For approving purchases? For on-boarding new clients or staff?

So why don't professionals have a process for getting referrals?

Part of it is the twisted logic that says "if I do a great job and provide great service, I *deserve* to get referrals. I don't need to ask because my clients will be only too happy to do it."

Part of it—and it follows from what I've just said—is the feeling that if we have to ask for referrals there must be something wrong with us: we "obviously" aren't good enough at what we do for clients to refer us of their own accord.

Finally, there's just not knowing what to do; how to approach the referral conversation.

The other side of the equation is the quality of referrals you get. Just now I described life in an ideal world: clients who are referred to you 'properly' will be less price resistant, easier to close, more likely to refer and more loyal.

Unfortunately, your existing clients don't always do a great job of referring you. The problem for them is that they don't know how to approach the conversation either. Most of the time, when someone says "do you know anyone who could do X for me?" their response is: "oh, you should talk to my X. She's great."

It's an OK referral—at least the person now knows you exist—but it's hardly a great referral.

And notice that their friend had to ask the question in order for them to make the referral in the first place: very few clients actually think to refer without being asked. Their job is to pay you, and they are doing that. Their job is not to sell your business for you.

So how do we make referrals easier? Your authority book.

When you have your book, the referral conversation with your clients is not "hey, do you know anyone who could use our services?" It's "hey, I've just released a book about what we do. I have a copy for you, and I thought you might like a few copies to give to anyone else you know who might benefit from reading it."

Notice: not "benefit from working with us", but "benefit from reading [the book]".

That's a much easier conversation to have.

Then they go to their friends. The conversation is no longer "Hi, I've been working with an X, and I think you ought to speak to them. Just say I sent you." Now it's "My lawyer literally wrote the book on property contracts. You really should read it. Have a copy." So now they're not having to sell you, they are just giving away a book.

And by giving away that book they get a double pay-off of pleasure. First they are helping a friend to solve a problem, which always feels good. Second, they get to say that they have been working with a published author, and everyone loves to have something they can brag about.

For the recipient, they have just received something of real value. Which would you rather receive: a book, or a brochure?

What if your client doesn't want to give their friends a book? Offer to send an autographed copy to anyone they nominate. They just need to give you the name and address of the recipient and you'll take care of the rest. You could even include a gift card written by them.

So how is that book going to turn into business? The calls to action we've already discussed. Your book will transform your business into one that really is built on 'word of mouth'.

Some of my best clients have been people who received a copy of one of my books from someone they trusted. And they in turn have gone on to use books to grow their business. Why? Because they had seen it work for themselves.

Maximise ROI On Advertising

There's a law firm in Toronto. They advertise every day in the breaks on the evening news. It must cost them a small fortune. Possibly not such a small one. At the end of the ad, the call to action is to call their office. There are three problems with that.

First, they are relying on someone being ready to call at that moment. Second, people know that if they call they are going to get sold to. Third, if the viewer is already working with a lawyer, they are unlikely to call.

Now, I'm not saying that you should start encouraging your competitors' clients to switch to you in your adverts, but about ten years ago a friend of mine was going through a particularly nasty divorce. He was unhappy with how his lawyer was handling things, but he was convinced that things couldn't be any different. He should have switched lawyers, and everyone around him kept telling him to, but he wouldn't budge. I can't help feeling that a book written by a local lawyer on how to maximise your divorce settlement might have convinced him where we failed.

Here's the point, though. People who aren't ready to call, or who don't feel like they can call because they are already talking to someone, or who are worried they are going to get sold to: they are not going to call, even if they see your ad on TV every day. But they *will* call to request a copy of a book.

Better Conversions From Mail Campaigns

Direct mail is making a comeback.

Sending things through the mail almost died out a few years ago. People were sick of receiving junk mail through their letter box, and companies realised they could send emails for free instead of paying to send unsolicited mail.

That was then.

Today, the backlash is against spam email. Every day I go through my inbox and delete dozens of emails unread, or at best barely skimmed. Email open rates are in the low single digits. Anti-Spam legislation is becoming more and more draconian. I live in Canada, which has laws which would make most business owners think twice before clicking send on a message to their own mother, let alone to a near stranger.

As a result, direct mail is making a comeback. We no longer receive a 6-inch tall pile of junk every day. When post arrives it's no longer such a chore to go through it. Indeed, getting something tangible through the mail triggers very positive associations, as we saw earlier, with holidays and gift giving.

Even Google has got in on the game. The owners of Gmail sent me a printed card through the mail with a voucher code to try their pay-per-click advertising. If Google thinks printed stuff in the post works, do you think you should try it too?

The challenge is to get people to act on what they receive. We've already discussed why suggesting people get in touch to claim a free report or a free consultation is unlikely to get much response. By the same token, inviting them to claim a free copy of a book will get a much higher response.

It's hard to think of a better lead generation offer than a printed book. Unlike pdfs, CDs, links to online videos or anything else, a book has a sense of importance and value. "Claim your free copy now" is irresistible.

As a way to get your envelope opened in the first place, "free book enclosed" is pretty hard to beat too. Who do you know who would throw out a free book (compared to throwing out a brochure or a letter)?

Closing The Complex Sale

The challenge many professionals face is that the services they sell are typically very complex, and hard for potential clients to understand, particularly if they have never bought anything of that type before.

Consulting projects, investment strategies, legal protection, financial management: they are all potentially complex sales.

If you're in that kind of business, you typically have three choices available to you.

1. You dumb down the service, or sell a cut down version. Either way you end up cutting down your fees at the same time.

2. You continue making complex pitches, and accept that your conversion rate is going to be lower than it could—and should—be
3. You stay away from offering truly complex packages altogether, and seriously hamper your ability to grow and reach the top levels of fees and the most interesting clients

A book will help you to get past the blocks that make complex sales difficult and close the deal faster and more easily.

The real problem with making complex sales is that the sales process can easily get out of control. Clients get bogged down in details that are possibly quite inconsequential, but the clients understand them so they can avoid looking at more important aspects that they don't fully understand. At the same time, the sales cycle gets strung out to become longer and longer. The problem is that the pace of change in business—indeed in the world at large—is accelerating. So if your sales process takes a long time the chances are that something is going to change, for you or for your clients. You end up having to change what you were pitching, or the client may even pull out altogether.

The result? Closing a complex sale becomes an expensive process. You are eating into your profits without even knowing whether you will get the sale. That's not a comfortable situation to be in.

> Many years ago, as a senior manager in one of the largest consulting firms in the world, I managed a multi-million-dollar pitch to a global corporation to implement a major new finance system and the accompanying processes. After

the first presentation we had an agreement in principle, and we were convinced we had got the client.

The next six months became a nightmare as we got pulled into more and more meetings with an ever-growing decision-making unit, and brought in more and more senior-level resources on our side. In that time, the requirements changed three times.

In the end we reduced our proposal to a feasibility study, for a fee that barely covered the costs of the pitch. Your sales may not be as extreme as this, but I'm sure you've seen similar situations.

A book can help you make the complex sale by handling many of the most common questions and objections your potential clients raise.

It allows you to explain what you do and how, in a medium that allows the client to review and reflect on it, check their understanding and move ahead at their own pace.

It allows you to communicate the big concepts and the big picture so that your clients are very clear on them before they get into a sales meeting.

During presentations you can refer back to what you say in the book, which makes the ideas seem more familiar and reminds them that they already know the answer to the questions they were about to ask.

After the sale, you can keep referring to the book during delivery so that the client understands where they are in the process, why things are being done the way they are, and what the endgame is. It makes delivery a much smoother and more pleasant experience for you and your staff, and for the client.

Higher Fees And Prices Thanks To A Higher-End Positioning In Your Market

In 'Premium! How Experts just Like You Are Charging Premium Fees For What They Know And You Can Too" I discussed how premium rates come from being positioned as an authority in your market.

One of the biggest challenges you face is that potential clients often find it difficult to distinguish between professionals based purely on their qualifications and titles. The sad fact is that in most professions, more than 90% of practitioners are mere commodities in the eyes of clients, and struggle to charge anything more than 'the going rate' for their services.

If you want to charge more, you need to be able to answer the question, "why should I hire you, over and above any of your competitors, why should I do whatever you ask me to do in order to become a client, and why should I pay whatever fee you are asking even though your competitors charge less?"

That is the essence of being positioned as what I call the Natural Expert in your field: the person everyone wants to work with, whatever it takes, and whatever it costs.

That position comes from demonstrating superior knowledge, superior experience and superior results *in the specific areas that your*

Authority!

potential clients are most concerned with. And an authority book is the perfect vehicle for doing that.

Authority books have allowed my clients to raise their fees and to increase the overall value of their customers.

If you too would like to raise your fees and raise the quality of the clients you are pursuing, an authority book is the best strategy I know to help you make that shift. So, let's look at how you could have your authority book in the hands of your ideal prospect in the next 45 days.

Are You Ready To Join The Ten Thousand Club?

Writing your own authority book will transform your business. In this book you have seen many examples of how business owners like you have used books to acquire more clients, raise fees, and accelerate their sales cycle.

In this book, you've seen experts who have

- Got themselves featured in the media and nominated for high-profile awards.
- Opened the door to key targets who had refused to meet with them in the past.
- Multiplied the lifetime value of their customers by factors of between 5 and 40.
- Closed five-figure deals in hours.
- Created six-figure income streams in weeks with virtually no list.

Authority!

They did this by becoming one of the one-in-ten thousand people on earth who have written a book: they have become members of The Ten Thousand Club.

Writing a book seems like a simple step to some professionals, a daunting mountain to climb to others. The reality is, it is the same as any other strategy for growing your business: you need a plan, with steps and deadlines, and you need to follow that plan. And often the best way to make sure you get through that plan is to work with someone who has done it before.

It is too easy to miss a step, or misjudge it, when you try to do something unfamiliar on your own.

Similarly, when it comes to promoting your book or getting it to the people who need to have it, you need a strategy, and probably a partner to help you implement it.

Where do you start?

Let me recap the process I have taken you through in this book, which I will represent as a series of questions.

1. **Why are you writing this book?** A book can help you achieve many business objectives, but it should focus on one. Do you want to use the book to launch a new business? Or to open up a new market? Do you want it to get you new clients? Or to generate new leads?
2. **Who needs to read your book?** While it is possible to write a book for a very general audience—indeed a traditional publisher will push you in that direction because they want book sales—you should write for your ideal target client.

Who that is will be informed by the answer to question 1, because in effect you need to ask yourself: if my objective is X, who do I need to get the book in front of to achieve that?

3. **What do you want them to do after reading your book?** Again, you are writing with a purpose for a specific audience. What action does your reader need to take to get you closer to your objective? Do you want them to call your office? Visit a physical location? Buy something? What do you need them to do?

4. **What does the reader need to know in order to do that?** Think about it. There is a reason your audience isn't already taking the steps you want them to, and that reason is some piece of knowledge they are lacking. If they had that knowledge they would immediately do what they need to do. It may be lack of knowledge of some particular opportunity or threat, or even lack of awareness of an entire field. It is rarely simply that they don't know you exist: if that was the case then brochures and business cards would be all the marketing you ever had to do. So list all the things your target audience would need to know in order for them to realise that you are the solution to their problem.

5. **How are you going to get your book written?** Choose the kind of book you are going to write. Is it a Panel of Experts book? An Interview With The Master? A Q&A Book? Review the chapter on writing your book and choose the format that best suits you and where your business currently is.

6. **How are you going to get your book into the hands of your audience?** Again, review the chapter on this topic and identify a range of different ways to get your book 'out there'.

In particular, choose something you can do to get your book out quickly, some strategies that are more medium term, and others that you can be preparing for but will be further in the future.

7. **How will you monetise your book?** Is this purely designed to be a book you follow up on to get people into a sales meeting? Or will you build products and services on the back of it? Plan your calls to action.

8. **Why would they read your book?** Writing is definitely not a case of 'if you write it they will read' (to paraphrase the well-known film). Your readers are likely to be busy people, so you need a powerful hook to get them to pick up your book and read it. If they don't get that far then they are not going to do anything, however many calls to action you put in the book. So you need to think about what is in it for the reader. "Finding out more about our products and services" isn't a tempting enough proposition for many people outside your immediate organisation.

9. **How will you launch the book?** One of the most valuable steps you can take in publishing your book is to do a planned launch campaign. Mainstream publishers tend to favour a launch party to which the author and publisher invite the press, key influencers and other valuable guests, with the aim of creating buzz around the new book. It's fun and feels great for a few days afterwards, but I prefer a far more pragmatic approach to launching our client's books. Our authors create bonus offers that are made available to buyers on condition that they buy within a certain time. That creates momentum which, when properly managed, can earn authors bestseller status on Amazon—and the only thing more powerful than

saying you are an author is being able to say that you are a best-selling author.

10. **What's next?** A book is rarely a business model on its own. You should think of it as part of a complex ecosystem designed to take people from strangers to referrers. You need to create an online platform that facilitates that journey. Your book will be a step along the path, but there will be other resources, meetings products and services along the way. One of the areas that we help our clients with is setting up a Sales Funnel and optimising your sales conversions. That is what turns an authority book into the cornerstone of a business.

Free Resource

I've created a guide to what we call 'the client journey'. To download a copy visit www.AuthorityExpertBook.com/register and register your copy of this book.

---

11. **The final step is to actually produce the book.** There is very little point in doing it before you have answered the first ten questions, because the last thing you want is to start writing your book and then realise that it is not 'fit for purpose' once you've figured out what that purpose is. So, only now should you start to plan content, the title and taglines, cover illustrations, blurb, and everything else you need to do to actually get the book into production.

Don't worry if the list seems overwhelming. In this book I have given you what you need to get started with creating your own authority book.

Looking for Help?

If you prefer not to embark on that journey alone, you can find out more about the programmes and services we provide at www.robcuesta.com/tenthousandclub

---

There you'll learn about our Write To Sell programme. Write To Sell offers you the opportunity to have your book written and on Amazon as early as next month. Imagine the opportunities you could create if, weeks from now, you were handing out a professionally produced book to your key targets, and having them call you instead of you having to constantly chase them. What doors would open if you approached them as a best-selling author rather than a thinly disguised salesperson? How would your standing in your profession and local community be enhanced if the media carried coverage of your newly released book?

Need help?

We are always looking for our next great success story, so if you think your authority book success story could be featured in an upcoming book, you can find out more about the programmes and services we provide at www.robcuesta.com/tenthousandclub

---

Testimonials

"We Have Six Leads In The Pipeline Each Worth $180,000 A Year"

Rob helped us develop a book to sell our concept. We had been chasing a key target for 3 years with no success, but one week after receiving our book they rang us. And they weren't alone. Now we have six leads in the pipeline each worth over $180,000. So if you're wondering whether to contact Rob, the answer is "yes"

Frank Butler, Chef In A Box Limited

"I Had 35% More Sales From My Current Business In The Last 6 Months"

Rob's programs have great value for anyone who wants to accelerate their business. Personally for me, I had about 35% more sales from my current business during the last 6 months.

Tadas Pakalnis

"I Unearthed $34,000 of Additional Revenue That I'd Previously Overlooked"

Suddenly I could see a way forward and the pieces of the jigsaw began to fall slowly into place; a clear step by step detailed action plan was shaped and formed, and I know I can realistically achieve the targets set. I also learned huge amounts about myself, but the icing on the cake was unearthing a potential £20,000 ($34k) of additional revenue that I'd previously ovelooked. So what about you? Are you going to wait for the 'business fairy' to come along and wave a magic wand or are you going to take responsibility for yourself – TODAY?

Allison Marlowe

"In Just 6 Months The Results Have Been Phenomenal"

Rob Cuesta's knowledge and mastery of his subject is always a pleasure to witness. In just under 6 months the results have been phenomenal: I have written and printed my first book, which is getting great reviews, and I've turned what I do into a programe that is much easier to pitch.

Alain Balanche-Jacquet

"I Can Spend More Time Earning Money"

Rob Cuesta has provided me with a clear, logical and effective blueprint on how to cut through all the confusing noise around marketing, both on-line and off-line. I have now been able to create a professional marketing strategy and put it on automatic so that rather than spend time struggling to find clients, I can spend more time earning money.

George Pirintzi

"Rob Clarified The Steps To Bring My Business To The Next Level"

Rob's expertise and models not only clarified the steps necessary to bring my business to the next level but it also helped clarify my vision and purpose. His humour, passion, integrity and knowledge shine through with every word. I highly recommend Rob to anyone looking to increase value in their business.

Len Benoit

About The Author

Rob Cuesta is an expert in online brand optimisation, sales funnel acceleration and customer value maximisation, based in Toronto, Canada.

Rob is the CEO and Principal Strategist of Joined-Up Marketing and HyperSuasion Consulting, and and the author of five best-selling books on marketing for professional practices. With a client base that spans four continents and over 25 years' experience as an award-winning speaker, consultant and marketer, Rob has worked with some of the largest organizations in the world, and some of the smallest.

Effective marketing comes down to three things: you need to position yourself, you need to create valuable offers, and you need to get paid.

"After completing my MBA at a top European business school, I realised that what was missing form a lot of the standard approaches to marketing was a way of showing a direct link from marketing to revenue. Business owners were screaming 'show me the money!' and marketers couldn't. Or wouldn't. So I made myself a promise: to only use marketing techniques—for myself and for my clients—that would directly drive money into the business."

Rob's promise is simple: to help you add an extra zero to your income by positioning yourself as the leading expert in your field and then developing marketing funnels that convert total strangers into buyers, repeat buyers, and ultimately into referrers. All on autopilot.

WARNING: working with Rob may expose you to revolutionary ideas, untapped revenue streams and extreme profitability. You have been warned!

You can also connect with me at the following places:

- Twitter: twitter.com/RobCuesta
- Facebook: facebook.com/joinedupmarketingworks
- LinkedIn: ca.linkedin.com/in/robcuesta/
- iTunes: http://0s4.com/r/JUMS
- YouTube: youtube.com/joinedupmarketingtv
- Google+:   http://0s4.com/r/JUMGP
- WWW: RobCuesta.com

Other Books By Rob Cuesta

If you've enjoyed this book you may also enjoy Rob's other books.

Rob's author page on Amazon.com:

http://www.amazon.com/author/robcuesta

Premium!

http://www.PremiumPricingBook.com

Secrets of a Six Figure Expert

Print: http://amzn.to/1rEKHMK

More Clients, More Money, More Fun

Kindle: http://amzn.to/1keyqwr

Acknowledgements

In the years since starting my own business, I have worked with, hired, studied and/or learned from many mentors and influencers from around the world. The list below can never hope to be comprehensive, and if I have missed someone out then I apologise, and hopefully I will realise the omission and correct it in future editions of this book.

For now, here goes.

Thank you for your wisdom, advice and support

- Andy Harrington
- Andy Jenkins
- Anthony Robbins
- Dan Bradbury
- Dan Kennedy
- Dave Vanhoose
- Dustin Matthews
- Ed Rush

- Jeff Walker
- Joanna Martin
- Jonathan Jay
- Mike Filsaime
- Mike Koenigs
- Paul Colligan
- Ryan Deiss

Further Reading

If you found this book interesting, you may also enjoy:

Mike Koenigs, Publish And Profit http://amzn.to/11YcDAG

Jeff Walker, Launch
http://amzn.to/1vly59D

Michael Hyatt, Platform
http://amzn.to/15Q8mkW

Dan Kennedy, Book The Business
http://amzn.to/1yoYnxH

Reader Bonuses

Remember!

Visit www.AuthorityExpertBook.com/register and confirm your purchase to get access to all the resources, guides and worksheets mentioned in this book.

Made in the USA
San Bernardino, CA
23 December 2014